EVERYDAY
Literacy

Listening & Speaking

Download Parent Letters in Spanish

Each week, there is a Home–School Connection Letter to send home with students. These letters are available in Spanish on our website.

How to Download:

1. Go to www.evan-moor.com/resources.

2. Enter your e-mail address and the resource code for this product—EMC2415.

3. You will receive an e-mail with a link to the downloadable letters, as well as an attachment with instructions.

Writing: Barbara Allman
Content Editing: Lisa Vitarisi Mathews
Leslie Sorg
Copy Editing: Carrie Gwynne
Art Direction: Cheryl Puckett
Cover Design: Cheryl Puckett
Illustration: Shirley Beckes
Design/Production: Carolina Caird
Yuki Meyer

EMC 2415

Evan-Moor®
EDUCATIONAL PUBLISHERS
Helping Children Learn since 1979

Congratulations on your purchase of some of the finest teaching materials in the world.

Correlated to State Standards

CPSIA: Worldcolor Dubuque, 2470 Kerper Boulevard, Dubuque, IA USA. 52001 [12/2009]

Contents

What's Inside?

In this book, you will find **20 weekly lessons**. Each weekly lesson includes:

3 Teacher Pages

Use these pages to guide you through the week.

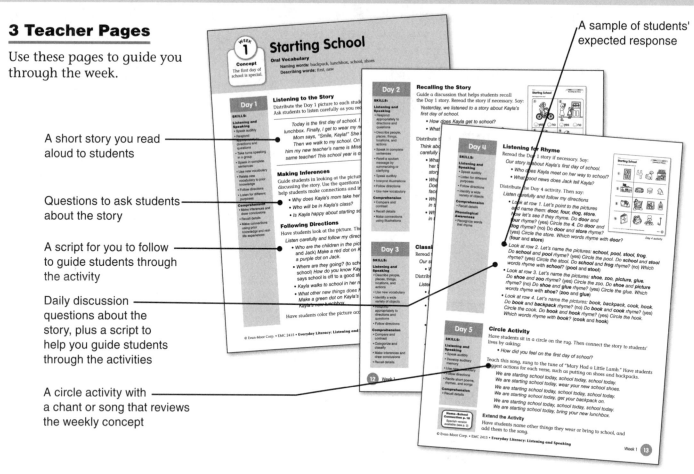

A short story you read aloud to students

Questions to ask students about the story

A script for you to follow to guide students through the activity

Daily discussion questions about the story, plus a script to help you guide students through the activities

A circle activity with a chant or song that reviews the weekly concept

A sample of students' expected response

4 Student Activity Pages

Reproduce each page for students to complete during the daily lesson.

1 Home–School Connection Page

At the end of each week, give students the **Home–School Connection** page (in English or Spanish) to take home.

To access the Spanish version of the activity, go to www.evan-moor.com/resources. Enter your e-mail address and the resource code EMC 2415.

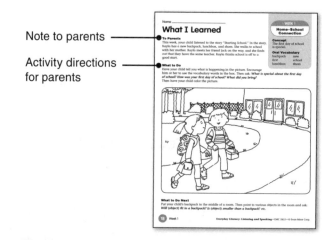

Note to parents

Activity directions for parents

How to Use This Book

Follow these easy steps to conduct the lessons:

Day 1

Reproduce and distribute the *Day 1 Student Page* to each student.

Using the scripted *Day 1 Teacher Page:*

1. Read the story aloud as students listen and look at the picture.

2. Discuss the story.

3. Have students complete the activity.

Days 2, 3, 4

Reproduce and distribute the appropriate day's activity page to each student.

Using the scripted *Teacher Page:*

1. Review the story from Day 1.

2. Discuss the story.

3. Have students complete the activity.

Day 5

Use the questions on the *Teacher Page* to guide a discussion about the story.

Follow the directions to lead the circle activity.

Send home the **Home–School Connection** page with each student.

Home–School Connection

Tips for Success

- Review the Teacher Page before you begin the lesson.

- Work with students in groups of 4 or 5 at a time.

- Have students sit at a table in a quiet area of the classroom.

- Model how to respond to questions using complete sentences.

- Allow students enough time to think about the question and to answer.

- To maintain students' attention, use basic hand signals:

   Put your hand to your ear to indicate that students should listen and not talk.

   Raise your hand in a "stop" signal to indicate that you want students to pay attention.

   Extend your hand (palm up) to one student to indicate it is his or her turn to answer a question.

Skills Chart

Week	Speak audibly	Take turns speaking in a group	Identify and sort common words into basic categories	Use positional words	Relate new vocabulary to prior knowledge	Describe ideas, feelings, and experiences	Speak in complete sentences	Describe people, places, things, locations, and actions	Respond appropriately to directions and questions	Retell a spoken message by summarizing or clarifying	Listen critically to interpret and evaluate	Understand and use words for categories	Use new vocabulary	Follow directions	Identify a wide variety of objects	Interpret illustrations	Recite short poems, rhymes, and songs	Listen for different purposes	Use language to show reasoning	Develop auditory memory	Make predictions	Make inferences and draw conclusions	Compare and contrast
Oral Language Development *(listening, speaking, and vocabulary)*																							
1	•	•			•		•	•	•	•			•	•	•		•	•		•		•	•
2	•	•		•			•	•	•				•	•		•	•	•	•	•		•	•
3	•	•			•	•	•		•		•		•	•		•			•			•	
4	•			•		•			•		•		•	•	•	•	•	•	•	•		•	
5	•	•			•	•	•		•				•	•		•			•	•		•	
6	•	•	•			•			•		•		•	•	•	•	•			•		•	
7	•	•					•		•		•		•	•	•	•	•	•	•	•		•	
8	•	•			•		•	•	•		•		•	•	•	•	•	•	•	•		•	
9	•	•			•		•		•			•	•	•	•	•	•	•	•	•		•	•
10	•	•			•	•	•		•	•			•	•	•	•				•	•	•	
11	•	•			•		•	•	•				•	•	•	•	•	•	•	•		•	
12	•	•	•		•	•	•	•	•				•	•		•			•	•		•	
13	•	•		•			•		•				•	•	•	•			•			•	
14	•	•	•		•		•		•				•	•	•	•	•	•	•	•		•	
15	•	•					•		•				•	•	•	•			•			•	
16	•	•			•	•	•	•	•				•	•	•	•			•	•	•	•	
17	•	•			•		•	•	•				•	•	•	•			•			•	
18	•	•			•		•		•				•	•	•	•			•	•		•	
19	•	•			•		•		•		•		•	•	•	•	•	•	•	•		•	
20	•	•			•	•	•	•	•				•	•	•	•	•	•	•	•	•	•	

Everyday Literacy: Listening and Speaking • EMC 2415 • © Evan-Moor Corp.

Distinguish between real and make-believe	Determine cause and effect	Categorize and classify	Identify a sequence of events	Identify beginning, middle, and end of a story	Recall details	Retell a story	Respond to open-ended questions	Make connections using illustrations, prior knowledge, and real-life experiences	Note details	Recognize words that rhyme	Identify examples of alliteration in spoken language	Identify common beginning and ending consonant sounds in spoken words	Identify medial short vowel sounds in spoken words	Identify medial long vowel sounds in spoken words	Identify common medial consonant sounds in spoken words	Perceive differences between similar-sounding spoken words	Repeat auditory sequences (e.g., letters, words, numbers, rhythmic patterns)	Syllables: blend when orally divided; syllabicate	Blend the sounds of an onset/rime of a spoken word	Break a spoken word into separate phonemes; count phonemes	Develop small muscle coordination	Develop large muscle coordination	Week
		•			•			•		•													1
			•		•	•		•	•												•	•	2
	•				•		•	•	•									•			•		3
					•		•	•				•											4
					•		•	•	•												•		5
		•			•			•	•										•		•		6
					•		•	•	•		•	•									•		7
			•		•		•		•			•									•		8
	•				•		•		•			•									•	•	9
					•		•		•	•		•									•	•	10
			•		•	•			•									•			•	•	11
	•				•		•		•											•			12
•		•			•		•		•	•											•	•	13
	•				•	•		•	•			•			•						•		14
					•		•	•	•					•							•		15
		•			•		•		•								•					•	16
					•				•				•			•					•		17
					•		•	•												•	•	•	18
		•			•			•	•											•	•		19
	•		•		•	•	•	•		•						•					•	•	20

© Evan-Moor Corp. • EMC 2415 • *Everyday Literacy: Listening and Speaking*

Use this record sheet periodically to check a student's progress.

Everyday Literacy
Listening and Speaking

K

Student Progress Record

Name: ____________________

Write dates and comments below the student's proficiency level.

1: Rarely demonstrates 0 – 25 %
2: Occasionally demonstrates 25 – 50 %
3: Usually demonstrates 50 – 75 %
4: Consistently demonstrates 75 – 100 %

Oral Language Development	1	2	3	4
Shows a steady increase in listening and speaking vocabulary				
Relates new vocabulary to prior knowledge				
Shows an increased ability to listen and understand				
Uses newly learned vocabulary on multiple occasions and in new contexts				
Follows directions				
Speaks in complete sentences with subject-verb agreement				

Comprehension

Makes connections using illustrations and photos, prior knowledge, real-life experiences				
Makes inferences and draws conclusions				
Retells a story in sequence				

Phonological Awareness

Identifies rhyming words				
Breaks words into syllables				
Recognizes beginning sounds in familiar words				

Everyday Literacy
Listening and Speaking

Students' Names:

Small Group Record Sheet

Write dates and comments about students' performance each week.

Week	Title	Comments
1	Starting School	
2	Apple Picking	
3	Making New Friends	
4	Fall Fun	
5	Winter Weather	
6	Spring Is Here	
7	A Summer Day	
8	In the Garden	
9	Insects and Spiders	
10	Fire Safety	
11	The Lion and the Mouse	
12	Family Picnic	
13	Jack and Jill	
14	My Five Senses	
15	Healthy Teeth	
16	Family Night	
17	The 100th Day of School	
18	Parts of a Tree	
19	Classroom Zoo	
20	A New Friend	

Dear Parent or Guardian,

As part of our focus on listening and speaking skills, I will be reading a story to your child each week. Every day, we will complete an activity that focuses on listening and speaking skills. The activities are fun and relate to concepts presented in the story.

At the end of each week, I will send home an activity page for you to complete with your child. The activity page includes a short summary of the story, the main concept of the week, a list of oral vocabulary words, and an activity for you and your child to do together.

Sincerely,

Estimado padre o tutor:

En nuestra clase, estamos aprendiendo a escuchar y hablar mejor. Con este fin, cada semana le leeré un cuento a su niño(a). Cada día, completaremos una actividad para practicar a escuchar y hablar mejor. Estas actividades, además de divertidas, se relacionan con los conceptos que se presentan en el mismo cuento.

Al final de cada semana, le enviaré una hoja que explica las actividades que puede realizar con su niño(a). La hoja contiene el resumen del cuento, el tema de la semana, una lista de palabras de vocabulario y una actividad para hacer en casa.

Sinceramente,

Concept
The first day of school is special.

Starting School

Oral Vocabulary

Naming words: backpack, lunchbox, school, shoes
Describing words: first, new

Day 1

SKILLS:

Listening and Speaking
- Speak audibly
- Respond appropriately to directions and questions
- Take turns speaking in a group
- Speak in complete sentences
- Use new vocabulary
- Relate new vocabulary to prior knowledge
- Follow directions
- Listen for different purposes

Comprehension
- Make inferences and draw conclusions
- Recall details
- Make connections using prior knowledge and real-life experiences

Listening to the Story

Distribute the Day 1 picture to each student. Then read aloud the story below. Ask students to listen carefully as you read.

Today is the first day of school. I have a new backpack and a new lunchbox. Finally, I get to wear my new school shoes!
Mom says, "Smile, Kayla!" She takes my picture.
Then we walk to my school. On the way, I see my friend Jack. I tell him my new teacher's name is Miss Devin. Guess what. Jack has the same teacher! This school year is off to a good start!

Making Inferences

Guide students in looking at the picture and discussing the story. Use the questions below to help students make connections and inferences.

- *Why does Kayla's mom take her picture?*
- *Who will be in Kayla's class?*
- *Is Kayla happy about starting school? Why?*

Following Directions

Have students look at the picture. Then say:
Listen carefully and follow my directions.

- *Who are the children in the picture?* (Kayla and Jack) *Make a red dot on Kayla and a purple dot on Jack.*
- *Where are they going?* (to school) *What special day is it?* (first day of school) *How do you know Kayla is happy about starting school?* (She says school is off to a good start.) *Make a brown dot on the school.*
- *Kayla walks to school in her new shoes. Make a red dot on her shoes.*
- *What other new things does Kayla have?* (a new backpack and lunchbox) *Make a green dot on Kayla's new backpack. Make a yellow dot on Kayla's new lunchbox.*

Have students color the picture according to the dots they made.

Day 1 picture

SKILLS:

Listening and Speaking
• Respond appropriately to directions and questions
• Describe people, places, things, locations, and actions
• Speak in complete sentences
• Retell a spoken message by summarizing or clarifying
• Speak audibly
• Interpret illustrations
• Follow directions
• Use new vocabulary

Comprehension
• Compare and contrast
• Recall details
• Make connections using illustrations

Recalling the Story

Guide a discussion that helps students recall the Day 1 story. Reread the story if necessary. Say:

Yesterday, we listened to a story about Kayla's first day of school.

> • *How does Kayla get to school?*
> • *What new things does Kayla have?*

Distribute the Day 2 activity. Then say:

Think about what happens in the story. Listen carefully and follow my directions.

> • *What do you see in box 1? (Kayla is riding her bike.) Does Kayla ride her bike in the story? Color the happy face for* **yes** *or the sad face for* **no**. (no)
>
> • *What do you see in box 2? (Kayla's mom is taking a picture of Kayla.) Does this happen in the story? Color the happy face for* **yes** *or the sad face for* **no**. (yes)
>
> • *What do you see in box 3? (Kayla is ready for school.) Does this happen in the story? Color the happy face for* **yes** *or the sad face for* **no**. (yes)
>
> • *What do you see in box 4? (Kayla is walking a dog.) Does this happen in the story? Color the happy face for* **yes** *or the sad face for* **no**. (no)

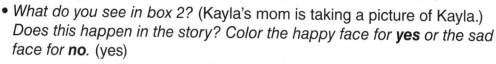

Day 2 activity

SKILLS:

Listening and Speaking
• Describe people, places, things, locations, and actions
• Use new vocabulary
• Identify a wide variety of objects
• Respond appropriately to directions and questions
• Follow directions

Comprehension
• Compare and contrast
• Categorize and classify
• Make inferences and draw conclusions
• Recall details

Classifying

Reread the Day 1 story if necessary. Say:

Our story is about Kayla's first day of school.

> • *What is Kayla happy about on the first day?*

Distribute the Day 3 activity. Then say:

Listen carefully and follow my directions.

> • *Point to the big picture on the page. What is it? (Kayla's new backpack)*
>
> • *Now look at the little pictures. Point to each one and name it with me. (chair, paper, flag, book, door, bike, pencil, crayons)*
>
> • *Let's help Kayla find things that will fit in her new backpack. Imagine these things are real. Which ones will fit in Kayla's backpack? (paper, book, pencil, crayons) Circle those things.*
>
> • *Which of these things would not fit in a backpack? (chair, flag, door, bike) Make an* **X** *on those things.*

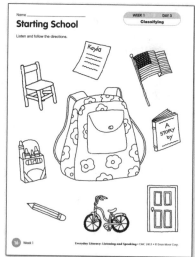

Day 3 activity

Day 4

SKILLS:

Listening and Speaking
• Speak audibly
• Listen for different purposes
• Follow directions
• Identify a wide variety of objects

Comprehension
• Recall details

Phonological Awareness
• Recognize words that rhyme

Listening for Rhyme

Reread the Day 1 story if necessary. Say:

Our story is about Kayla's first day of school.

> • *Who does Kayla meet on her way to school?*
>
> • *What good news does Jack tell Kayla?*

Distribute the Day 4 activity. Then say:

Listen carefully and follow my directions

Day 4 activity

> • *Look at row 1. Let's point to the pictures and name them: **door, four, dog, store**. Now let's see if they rhyme. Do **door** and **four** rhyme? (yes) Circle the **4**. Do **door** and **dog** rhyme? (no) Do **door** and **store** rhyme? (yes) Circle the store. Which words rhyme with **door**? (**four** and **store**)*
>
> • *Look at row 2. Let's name the pictures: **school, pool, stool, frog**. Do **school** and **pool** rhyme? (yes) Circle the pool. Do **school** and **stool** rhyme? (yes) Circle the stool. Do **school** and **frog** rhyme? (no) Which words rhyme with **school**? (**pool** and **stool**)*
>
> • *Look at row 3. Let's name the pictures: **shoe, zoo, picture, glue**. Do **shoe** and **zoo** rhyme? (yes) Circle the zoo. Do **shoe** and **picture** rhyme? (no) Do **shoe** and **glue** rhyme? (yes) Circle the glue. Which words rhyme with **shoe**? (**zoo** and **glue**)*
>
> • *Look at row 4. Let's name the pictures: **book, backpack, cook, hook**. Do **book** and **backpack** rhyme? (no) Do **book** and **cook** rhyme? (yes) Circle the cook. Do **book** and **hook** rhyme? (yes) Circle the hook. Which words rhyme with **book**? (**cook** and **hook**)*

Day 5

SKILLS:

Listening and Speaking
• Speak audibly
• Develop auditory memory
• Use new vocabulary
• Follow directions
• Recite short poems, rhymes, and songs

Comprehension
• Recall details

Circle Activity

Have students sit in a circle on the rug. Then connect the story to students' lives by asking:

> • *How did you feel on the first day of school?*

Teach this song, sung to the tune of "Mary Had a Little Lamb." Have students suggest actions for each verse, such as putting on shoes and backpacks.

> *We are starting school today, school today, school today.*
> *We are starting school today, wear your new school shoes.*
>
> *We are starting school today, school today, school today.*
> *We are starting school today, get your backpack on.*
>
> *We are starting school today, school today, school today.*
> *We are starting school today, bring your new lunchbox.*

Extend the Activity

Have students name other things they wear or bring to school, and add them to the song.

Home–School Connection p. 18
Spanish version available (see p. 2)

Name _____

Starting School

Everyday Literacy: Listening and Speaking • EMC 2415 • © Evan-Moor Corp.

Name _____

Starting School

Did it happen in the story?

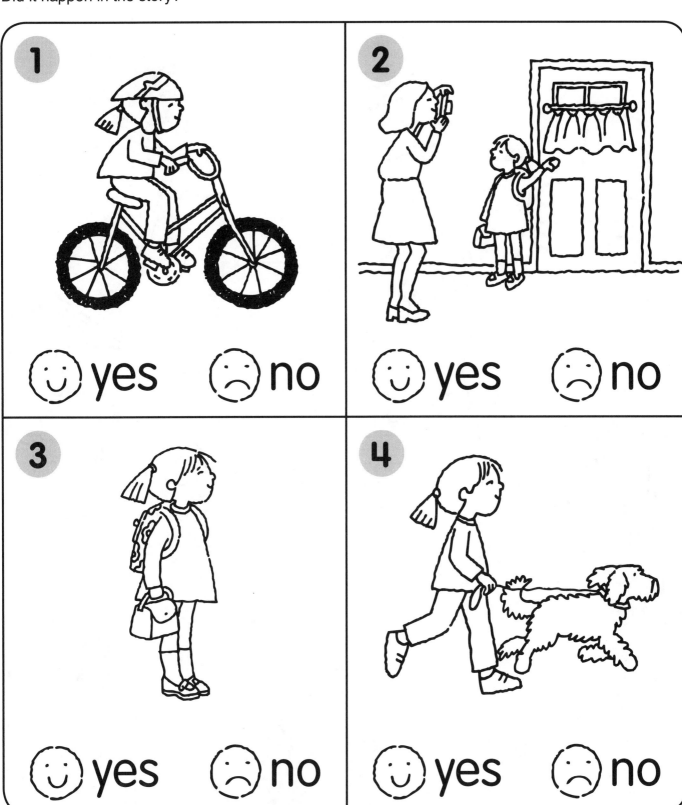

1. ☺ yes   ☹ no

2. ☺ yes   ☹ no

3. ☺ yes   ☹ no

4. ☺ yes   ☹ no

Name _____

Starting School

Listen and follow the directions.

Everyday Literacy: Listening and Speaking • EMC 2415 • © Evan-Moor Corp.

Name _____

Starting School

Circle the rhyming words in each row.

1
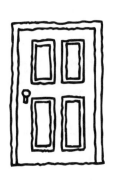   

2

3

4

Name _____

What I Learned

To Parents

This week, your child listened to the story "Starting School." In the story, Kayla has a new backpack, lunchbox, and shoes. She walks to school with her mother. Kayla meets her friend Jack on the way, and she finds out that they have the same teacher. Kayla thinks school is off to a good start.

What to Do

Have your child tell you what is happening in the picture. Encourage him or her to use the vocabulary words in the box. Then ask: *What is special about the first day of school? How was your first day of school? What did you bring?* Then have your child color the picture.

Concept
The first day of school is special.

Oral Vocabulary

backpack	new
first	school
lunchbox	shoes

What to Do Next

Put your child's backpack in the middle of a room. Then point to various objects in the room and ask: *Will* (object) *fit in a backpack? Is* (object) *smaller than a backpack?* etc.

Everyday Literacy: Listening and Speaking • EMC 2415 • © Evan-Moor Corp.

Concept

An apple is a fruit that grows on a tree.

Apple Picking

Oral Vocabulary

Naming words: apple, fruit, tree
Action word: pick
Describing words: green, red

Day 1

SKILLS:

Listening and Speaking
- Take turns speaking in a group
- Speak audibly
- Relate new vocabulary to prior knowledge
- Speak in complete sentences
- Use new vocabulary
- Interpret illustrations
- Listen for different purposes
- Respond appropriately to directions and questions
- Describe people, places, things, locations, and actions
- Follow directions

Comprehension
- Make inferences and draw conclusions
- Recall details
- Note details
- Make connections using illustrations, prior knowledge, and real-life experiences

Listening to the Story

Distribute the Day 1 picture to each student. Then read aloud the story below. Ask students to listen carefully as you read.

My friend John has two fruit trees in his backyard. Both of them are apple trees. John's mom said the apples are ready to pick. The big apple tree grows green apples. The little apple tree grows red apples. I picked one apple off the big tree. John picked one off the little tree. Then we ate our apples! Apples are my favorite fruit.

Making Inferences

Guide students in looking at the picture and discussing the story. Use the questions below to help students make connections and inferences.

- *What do apples grow on?*
- *John picked an apple from the little tree. Which color apple did John pick?*
- *Which color apple did the other boy pick?*
- *An apple is a fruit. What other fruits can you name?*

Day 1 picture

Following Directions

Have students look at the picture Then say:

Listen carefully and follow my directions.

- *What is in the basket?* (apples) *Make a yellow dot on the basket.*
- *Where do apples come from?* (They grow on apple trees.) *Make a brown dot on each tree. How many apple trees are there?* (two)
- *What color were the apples in the story?* (red and green) *Make green dots on the apples growing on the big tree. Make red dots on the apples growing on the little tree.*
- *What are the boys doing in the picture?* (They are picking apples.) *What color apple do you like to eat?* (Answers vary.) *Make a purple dot on one boy. Make an orange dot on his friend.*

Have students color the picture according to the dots they made.

Day 2

SKILLS:

Listening and Speaking
- Take turns speaking in a group
- Speak audibly
- Relate new vocabulary to prior knowledge
- Use new vocabulary
- Follow directions
- Interpret illustrations
- Listen for different purposes

Comprehension
- Make connections using illustrations and prior knowledge
- Retell a story
- Recall details
- Note details
- Identify a sequence of events

Sequencing

Guide a discussion that helps students recall the Day 1 story. Reread the story if necessary. Say:

In our story, two friends picked apples.

- *What does John have in his backyard?*

Distribute the Day 2 activity. Then say:

Listen carefully to this story: "John picks the apples from the trees. He puts them in a basket. Then he chooses one to eat. It is sweet and crunchy. All that is left is the core!"

- *Look at the pictures. Which one shows what John does first?* (John picking the apples) *Draw a line from the picture to the number* **1**.

- *Which picture shows what John does with the apples after he picks them?* (apples in the basket) *Draw a line from the picture to the number* **2**.

- *Which picture shows what John does after he finishes picking the apples?* (John eating an apple) *Draw a line from the picture to the number* **3**. *How do you think the apple tastes?* (Answers vary.)

- *One of the pictures shows how the apple looked when John finished eating it. This part of the apple is called the core. Draw a line from the core to the number* **4**.

Have students use the pictures to retell the story to a partner.

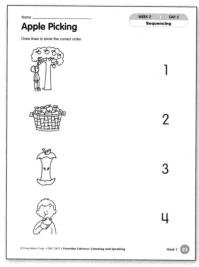

Day 2 activity

Day 3

SKILLS:

Listening and Speaking
- Speak audibly
- Describe people, places, things, locations, and actions
- Follow directions

Comprehension
- Recall details
- Note details
- Make connections using illustrations, prior knowledge, and real-life experiences

Motor Skills
- Develop small muscle coordination

Finishing a Picture

Reread the Day 1 story if necessary. Say:

In our story, two friends picked apples.

- *Where do apples come from?*

Distribute the Day 3 activity. Then say:

Listen carefully and follow my directions.

- *This picture of an apple tree isn't finished. Trace the line to finish the top of the apple tree. What color should the top of the apple tree be? What color are the leaves?* (green) *Color the top of the tree green.*

- *Next, connect the dots to make the trunk for the apple tree. Begin on* **1**. *Which numbers do you go to next?* (**2, 3, 4, 5**) *What color should the trunk be?* (brown) *Color the trunk brown.*

- *Draw three apples growing on the tree. What color apples do you like to eat?* (Answers vary.) *Color the apples.*

- *Pretend that one apple has fallen from the tree. Draw it on the grass.*

Day 3 activity

Everyday Literacy: Listening and Speaking • EMC 2415 • © Evan-Moor Corp.

Day 4

SKILLS:

Listening and Speaking
- Use positional words
- Take turns speaking in a group
- Speak audibly
- Use new vocabulary
- Describe people, places, things, locations, and actions
- Follow directions
- Listen for different purposes
- Use language to show reasoning

Comprehension
- Compare and contrast
- Note details
- Recall details

Identifying Differences

Reread the Day 1 story if necessary. Say:

This week, our story was about two friends who picked apples.

- *What did the boys pick the apples from?*
- *What color apples did they pick?*

Distribute the Day 4 activity. Then say:

- *Look at the apples in row 1. Point to the apple that is different. Why is it different? (It's been eaten. It's just a core.) Draw a circle around the apple that has been eaten.*
- *Look at the trees in row 2. What kind of trees are they? (apple) Point to the tree that is different. Why is it different? (The apples are not on the tree.) Draw a circle around the tree with apples under it.*
- *Look at the baskets in row 3. Point to the basket that is different. Why is it different? (It has apples in it.) What do the other baskets have in them? (nothing) Draw a circle around the basket with apples in it.*
- *Look at the pictures in row 4. Point to the boy who is different. What is different about him? (He is not eating an apple.) Draw a circle around the boy who does not have an apple.*

Day 4 activity

Day 5

SKILLS:

Listening and Speaking
- Recite short poems, rhymes, and songs
- Listen for different purposes
- Use new vocabulary
- Take turns speaking in a group
- Develop auditory memory

Comprehension
- Recall details

Motor Skills
- Develop large muscle coordination

Circle Activity

Have students sit in a circle on the rug. Then review the concepts and vocabulary they practiced this week. Ask:

- *What kind of food is an apple?*
- *What other fruits can we name?*

Introduce and model the chant below by reading it aloud and having the class echo you.

Apples are crunchy and sweet.
Apples are good to eat.

Then have students name other fruits to substitute in the chant. Help them replace the words **crunchy** and **sweet** with other appropriate adjectives (e.g., "Bananas are soft and squishy." or "Lemons are juicy and sour.").

Extend the Activity

Turn the chant into a game. Recite the chant, and roll a ball to a student. Have the student catching the ball repeat the rhyme and roll the ball to another student. Continue playing until each student has a chance to roll the ball and recite the chant.

Home–School Connection p. 26
Spanish version available (see p. 2)

Name _____

Apple Picking

Everyday Literacy: Listening and Speaking • EMC 2415 • © Evan-Moor Corp.

Name _____

Apple Picking

Draw lines to show the correct order.

1

2

3

4

Apple Picking

Listen and follow the directions to finish the picture.

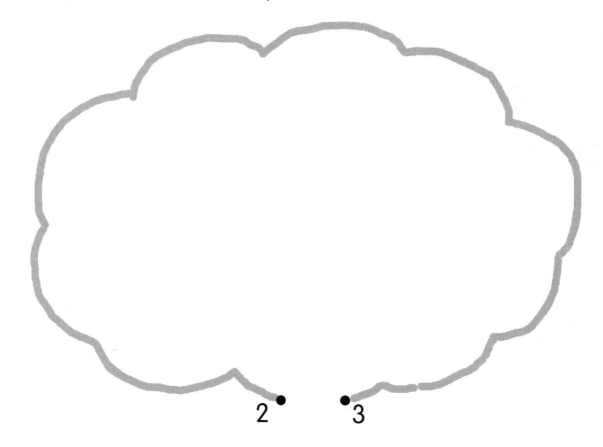

Name _____

Apple Picking

Circle the one that is different.

1

2
   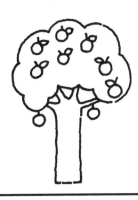

3

4

Name _____

What I Learned

To Parents

This week, your child listened to the story "Apple Picking." In the story, two friends picked apples. One boy picked green apples. The other boy picked red apples. They learned that apples grow on trees and are fruit.

What to Do

Have your child tell you what is happening in the picture. Ask questions such as: *Where do apples come from? What colors of apples have you seen? What is your favorite color of apple to eat? Can you name any other fruits?* Then have your child color the picture.

Concept

An apple is a fruit that grows on a tree.

Oral Vocabulary

apple	pick
fruit	red
green	tree

What to Do Next

Take your child to the grocery store or market. Point out the names of different varieties and colors of apples. Take home a variety of apples to taste. Ask your child to name his or her favorite.

Everyday Literacy: Listening and Speaking • EMC 2415 • © Evan-Moor Corp.

Concept

It is important to welcome new students.

Making New Friends

Oral Vocabulary

Naming words: class, classroom, school, turtle
Action word: welcome

Day 1

SKILLS:

Listening and Speaking
• Take turns speaking in a group
• Describe ideas, feelings, and experiences
• Use new vocabulary
• Relate new vocabulary to prior knowledge
• Follow directions
• Respond appropriately to directions and questions
• Use langue to show reasoning
• Speak audibly
• Speak in complete sentences
• Interpret illustrations

Comprehension
• Determine cause and effect
• Make inferences and draw conclusions
• Note details
• Recall details
• Make connections using illustrations and prior knowledge
• Respond to open-ended questions

Listening to the Story

Distribute the Day 1 picture to each student. Then read aloud the story below. Ask students to listen carefully as you read.

Today was my first day at a new school. The class came to the office to meet me. They said, "Welcome, Emily!" Then they showed me the way to my new classroom. When we got there, I had a big surprise. My new classmates showed me our class pet! I think I'm going to like this school.

Making Inferences

Guide students in looking at the picture and discussing the story. Use the questions below to help students make connections and inferences.

• *What did the class do to welcome Emily?*
• *What was the surprise?*
• *Why do you think Emily is going to like her new school?*
• *How would you make a new student feel welcome?*

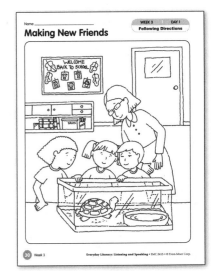

Day 1 picture

Following Directions

Have students look at the picture. Then say:

Listen carefully and follow my directions.

• *Where are the students?* (in their classroom) *How do you know this is a classroom?* (Answers vary.) *Do you see anything in the picture that we have in our classroom?* (Answers vary.) *Circle those things in the picture.*

• *What are the students doing?* (looking at the class pet) *What kind of animal is the class pet?* (a turtle) *Make a green dot on the turtle. Make a blue dot on each student.*

• *Who else is in the picture?* (the teacher) *How do you think she made Emily feel welcome?* (Answers vary.) *Make a red dot on the teacher.*

Have students color the picture according to the dots they made.

SKILLS:

Listening and Speaking
• Follow directions
• Relate new vocabulary to prior knowledge
• Describe ideas, feelings, and experiences

Comprehension
• Make connections using illustrations and prior knowledge
• Recall details
• Make inferences and draw conclusions

Motor Skills
• Develop small muscle coordination

Following Directions

Guide a discussion that helps students recall the Day 1 story. Reread the story if necessary. Say:

We listened to a story about a girl's first day at a new school.

> • *How did the class welcome Emily?*
>
> • *Do you think Emily will make friends?*

Distribute the Day 2 activity. Then say:

Emily and a new friend went outside to play during recess. Let's draw a path to show what they did. Listen carefully and follow my directions.

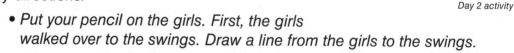

Day 2 activity

> • *Put your pencil on the girls. First, the girls walked over to the swings. Draw a line from the girls to the swings.*
>
> • *Next, the girls wanted to play ball. Draw a line from the swings to the ball.*
>
> • *Then, the girls decided to play with trucks in the sandbox. Draw a line from the ball to the sandbox.*
>
> • *After that, they wanted to play on the monkey bars. Draw a line from the sandbox to the monkey bars.*
>
> • *Finally, the bell rang and it was time to go back inside. Draw a line from the monkey bars to the doors.*
>
> • *Use the path you drew to tell a partner what Emily and her friend did during recess.*

SKILLS:

Listening and Speaking
• Follow directions
• Listen critically to interpret and evaluate
• Speak audibly

Comprehension
• Recall details

Phonological Awareness
• Break words into syllables

Counting Syllables

Reread the Day 1 story if necessary. Say:

Our story was about Emily and her new school.

> • *What did the class say to Emily?*
>
> • *What did the class show Emily?*

Distribute the Day 3 activity. Then say:

Day 3 activity

> • *Find the turtle. Say the word **turtle** and clap with me: **tur•tle**. How many word parts do you hear?* (two) *Circle **2**.*
>
> • *Find the school. Say the word **school** and clap with me: **school**. How many word parts do you hear?* (one) *Circle **1**.*
>
> • *Find Emily's classmates. Say the word **classmates** and clap with me: **class•mates** How many word parts do you hear?* (two) *Circle **2**.*
>
> • *Find Emily. Say the word **Emily** and clap with me: **Em•i•ly**. How many word parts do you hear?* (three) *Circle **3**.*

Have students color the pictures.

Everyday Literacy: Listening and Speaking • EMC 2415 • © Evan-Moor Corp.

Day 4

SKILLS:

Listening and Speaking
- Take turns speaking in a group
- Follow directions
- Respond appropriately to directions and questions
- Interpret illustrations
- Speak in complete sentences

Comprehension
- Recall details
- Make connections using illustrations, prior knowledge, and real-life experiences

Identifying Pictures

Reread the Day 1 story if necessary. Say:

This week, our story was about a girl on her first day at a new school.

- *Why should we make friends with children who are new to our school?*
- *What do you do to make friends?*

Distribute the Day 4 activity. Then say:

This activity is about how friends treat each other. Listen carefully and follow my directions.

- *What do you see in box 1?* (children building a tower with blocks) *Should friends help each other? Circle the happy face for* **yes** *or the sad face for* **no**. (yes)

- *What do you see in box 2?* (a boy giving a lollipop to another boy) *Should friends share? Circle the happy face for* **yes** *or the sad face for* **no**. (yes)

- *What do you see in box 3?* (a boy pulling a girl's hair) *Should friends pull hair? Circle the happy face for* **yes** *or the sad face for* **no**. (no)

- *What do you see in box 4?* (children waiting their turn to get a drink of water) *Should friends take turns? Circle the happy face for* **yes** *or the sad face for* **no**. (yes)

Day 4 activity

Day 5

SKILLS:

Listening and Speaking
- Recite short poems, rhymes, and songs
- Develop auditory memory

Comprehension
- Recall details
- Respond to open-ended questions

Circle Activity

Have students sit in a circle on the rug. Then review the concepts and vocabulary they practiced this week. Ask:

- *How did the class welcome Emily?*
- *How can you make friends with someone?*

Introduce and model the song below, sung to the tune of "The More We Get Together."

We make new friends feel welcome, feel welcome, feel welcome. We make new friends feel welcome. It's the right thing to do.

Chorus:
For new friends are great friends, yes new friends are great frier[ ] We make new friends feel welcome. It's the right thing to do.

Extend the Activity

Have students suggest other things they can do to welcome new[ ]us class. Use those ideas to create new verses for the song (e.g., "W[ ] our classroom..." or "We always speak with kind words..."). [ ] after each verse.

Home–School Connection p. 34
Spanish version available (see p. 2)

3 **29**

Name _____

Making New Friends

Name _____

Making New Friends

Listen and follow the directions.

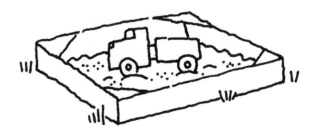

© Evan-Moor Corp. • EMC 2415 • *Everyday Literacy: Listening and Speaking*   Week 3   31

Name _____

Making New Friends

How many word parts do you hear?

1   2   3

1   2   3

1   2   3

1   2   3

Everyday Literacy: Listening and Speaking • EMC 2415 • © Evan-Moor Corp.

Name _____

Making New Friends

Is this what friends do?

1   ☺ yes   ☹ no

2   ☺ yes   ☹ no

3   ☺ yes   ☹ no

4   ☺ yes   ☹ no

Name _____

What I Learned

To Parents

This week, your child listened to the story "Making New Friends." In the story, it was Emily's first day at a new school. Her new class welcomed her. The students met her in the office and showed her the way to the classroom. They also showed Emily the class pet—a turtle! Emily thinks she will like her new school.

Concept
It is important to welcome new students.

Oral Vocabulary
class   turtle
classroom   welcome
school

What to Do

Have your child tell you what is happening in the picture. Ask questions such as: *How did the class welcome Emily? What are the students looking at in the picture? Do you think Emily will like her new school? How do you welcome new students to your class?* Then have your child color the picture.

What to Do Next

Ask your child to tell you how he or she would feel on the first day at a new school.

Everyday Literacy: Listening and Speaking • EMC 2415 • © Evan-Moor Corp.

Fall Fun

Oral Vocabulary

Naming words: fall, leaves, season, squirrel

Describing words: in, off, on, under

Day 1

SKILLS:

Listening and Speaking
- Take turns speaking in a group
- Use new vocabulary
- Use language to show reasoning
- Speak audibly
- Follow directions
- Relate new vocabulary to prior knowledge
- Respond appropriately to directions and questions
- Interpret illustrations
- Listen for different purposes

Comprehension
- Make inferences and draw conclusions
- Make connections using illustrations, prior knowledge, and real-life experiences
- Note details
- Recall details
- Respond to open-ended questions

Listening to the Story

Distribute the Day 1 picture to each student. Say: *There are four seasons, or parts of the year. Each one is different. Fall is a season.* Then read aloud the story below. Ask students to listen carefully as you read.

It is fall. A cool wind is blowing. My dog Quigley and I always check the weather before we go out to play. Today, red, yellow, and brown leaves are falling off the trees.

"Oh, look! There is a squirrel sitting on my pumpkin. Come on, Quigley! Let's go play in the leaves!"

Making Inferences

Guide students in looking at the picture and discussing the story. Use the questions below to help students make connections and inferences.

- *Which season is it?*
- *What is the weather like in fall?*
- *Where is the girl going?*
- *Why do you think the girl checks the weather before she goes outside to play?*
- *What is falling off the trees?*

Following Directions

Have students look at the picture. Then say:

Listen carefully and follow my directions.

- *How is the girl dressed for fall?* (jacket, pants) *Why does she wear a jacket and pants?* (There is a cool wind blowing.) *Make a red dot on her jacket. Make a blue dot on her pants.*
- *Who is Quigley?* (her dog) *What other animal do you see in the picture?* (squirrel) *Make a black dot on Quigley. Make a brown dot on the squirrel.*
- *What color is a pumpkin?* (orange) *Make an orange dot on the pumpkin.*
- *What colors are the leaves in fall?* (red, yellow, brown) *Make some red, yellow, and brown dots on the leaves.*

Have students color the picture according to the dots they made.

Day 1 picture

SKILLS:

Listening and Speaking
· Speak audibly
· Take turns speaking in a group
· Interpret illustrations
· Respond appropriately to directions and questions
· Speak in complete sentences
· Use new vocabulary

Comprehension
· Make inferences and draw conclusions
· Note details
· Recall details
· Make connections using illustrations, prior knowledge, and real-life experiences

Identifying Pictures

Guide a discussion that helps students recall the Day 1 story. Reread the story if necessary. Say:

Our story is about a girl and her dog.

- *Which season is it?*
- *What does the girl wear?*
- *What does the girl see outside?*

Distribute the Day 2 activity. Then say:

Listen carefully and follow my directions.

- *Look at box 1. In fall, the leaves on trees change colors. Then the leaves fall off the trees. Is it fall in the picture? Color the happy face for **yes** or the sad face for **no**.* (yes)

- *Look at box 2. In fall, squirrels hide nuts to eat during winter. Is it fall in the picture? Color the happy face for **yes** or the sad face for **no**.* (yes)

- *Look at box 3. In fall, children wear jackets and pants. The weather is cool. Is it fall in the picture? Color the happy face for **yes** or the sad face for **no**.* (no)

- *Look at box 4. In fall, people rake the leaves that fall off the trees. Is it fall in the picture? Color the happy face for **yes** or the sad face for **no**.* (yes)

Day 2 activity

SKILLS:

Listening and Speaking
· Identify a wide variety of objects
· Use positional words
· Interpret illustrations
· Listen critically to interpret and evaluate
· Take turns speaking in a group
· Follow directions
· Respond appropriately to directions and questions

Comprehension
· Recall details

Using Positional Words

Reread the Day 1 story if necessary. Say:

We listened to a story about fall.

- *Where do the girl and Quigley go?*
- *What colors are the leaves on the ground?*

Distribute the Day 3 activity. Then say:

Listen carefully and follow my directions.

- *Look at box 1. Circle the picture of the girl standing **in** the basket.*

- *Look at box 2. Circle the picture of the squirrel sitting **on** the fence.*

- *Look at box 3. Circle the picture of the leaves falling **off** the tree.*

- *Look at box 4. Circle the picture of the dog that is **under** the basket. Underline the picture of the dog jumping **over** the basket.*

- *Now look at each box again and tell about the picture you did not circle (e.g., The girl is **next to** the basket.)*

Day 3 activity

Everyday Literacy: Listening and Speaking • EMC 2415 • © Evan-Moor Corp.

Day 4

SKILLS:

Listening and Speaking
- Identify a wide variety of objects
- Listen for different purposes
- Follow directions
- Respond appropriately to directions and questions
- Listen critically to interpret and evaluate

Comprehension
- Recall details

Phonological Awareness
- Identify common ending consonant sounds in spoken words

Listening for Ending Sounds

Reread the Day 1 story if necessary. Say:

This week, our story is about fall.

- *Why does the girl check the weather before going outside to play?*
- *What is the squirrel sitting on?*

Distribute the Day 4 activity. Then say:

Listen carefully and follow my directions.

- *Look at row 1. Name the first picture.* (**nut**) *What is the ending sound in* **nut**? (**/t/**) *Let's find the picture with the same ending sound: nut–pig, nut–cat.* **Nut** *and* **cat** *have the same ending sound. Circle the cat.*

- *Look at row 2. Name the first picture.* (**leaf**) *What is the ending sound in* **leaf**? (**/f/**) *Let's find the picture with the same ending sound: leaf–fish, leaf–scarf.* **Leaf** *and* **scarf** *have the same ending sound. Circle the scarf.*

- *Look at row 3. Name the first picture.* (**wind**) *What is the ending sound in* **wind**? (**/d/**) *Let's find the picture with the same ending sound: wind–bat, wind–bed.* **Wind** *and* **bed** *have the same ending sound. Circle the bed.*

- *Look at row 4. Name the first picture.* (**dog**) *What is the ending sound in* **dog**? (**/g/**) *Let's find the picture with the same ending sound: dog–bag, dog–jacket.* **Dog** *and* **bag** *have the same ending sound. Circle the bag.*

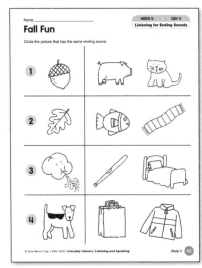

Day 4 activity

Day 5

SKILLS:

Listening and Speaking
- Recite short poems, rhymes, and songs
- Respond appropriately to directions and questions
- Develop auditory memory
- Use new vocabulary

Comprehension
- Recall details

Home–School Connection p. 42
Spanish version available (see p. 2)

Circle Activity

Have students sit in a circle on the rug. Then review the concepts and vocabulary they practiced this week. Ask:

- *What is the weather like in fall?*
- *What happens to trees in fall?*

Introduce and model the song below, sung to the tune of "Mary Had a Little Lamb." Sing each line and have the class echo you. Then sing the verses together.

Leaves are falling everywhere, everywhere, everywhere.
Leaves are falling everywhere, because it's fall.

There's a cool wind blowing, … etc.

There's a squirrel saving nuts, … etc.

Leaves are turning red and brown,… etc.

Extend the Activity

Have students draw pictures of what they like to do in fall.

Fall Fun

Everyday Literacy: Listening and Speaking • EMC 2415 • © Evan-Moor Corp.

Name _____

Fall Fun

Listen and follow the directions.

 yes no

yes no

yes no

yes no

Name _____

Fall Fun

Listen and follow the directions.

Fall Fun

Circle the picture that has the same ending sound.

1

2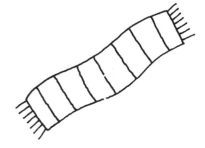

3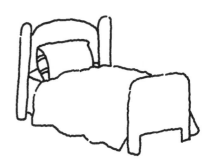

4

Name _____

What I Learned

Concept
Fall is a season.

Oral Vocabulary

fall	on
in	season
leaves	squirrel
off	under

To Parents

This week, your child listened to the story "Fall Fun." In the story, a girl and her dog check the weather before they go outside to play. When they look outside, they feel the cool fall air and see red, yellow, and brown leaves falling off the trees. Then they see a squirrel sitting on a pumpkin. The girl and her dog go outside to play in the leaves.

What to Do

Explain that this is a picture about fall. Have your child tell you about the picture. Ask questions such as: *How do you know it is fall in the picture? What is the weather like in fall? What should the girl be wearing? Where is the squirrel? What do squirrels do in fall?* Have your child draw a jacket on the girl and a nut for the squirrel. Then have him or her finish coloring the picture.

What to Do Next

Go for a walk outside together and collect leaves. Place the leaves between sheets of newspaper, and put a heavy book or a pile of magazines on top to flatten the leaves. After a day or two, remove the leaves and look at them with your child. Have him or her describe how the leaves are alike and how they are different.

Everyday Literacy: Listening and Speaking • EMC 2415 • © Evan-Moor Corp.

Winter Weather

Oral Vocabulary

Naming words: boots, coat, hat, mittens, scarf, snow, winter

Day 1

SKILLS:

Listening and Speaking
• Speak audibly
• Take turns speaking in a group
• Respond appropriately to directions and questions
• Follow directions
• Interpret illustrations
• Listen for different purposes
• Speak in complete sentences
• Use new vocabulary

Comprehension
• Respond to open-ended questions
• Make inferences and draw conclusions
• Make connections using illustrations, prior knowledge, and real-life experiences
• Note details
• Recall details

Listening to the Story

Distribute the Day 1 picture to each student. Say: *There are four seasons. Each one is different. Winter is a season.* Then read aloud the story below. Ask students to listen carefully as you read.

"Yippee! It's snowing," said Mike. He asked his mom if he could go next door to see if his friend Jesse could come out and play.

Mom said, "Put on your winter clothes."

"Okay, Mom," said Mike.

So Mike put on his coat, his hat, his boots, and his mittens. But he couldn't find his scarf. Where did he leave it?

Making Inferences

Guide students in looking at the picture and discussing the story. Use the questions below to help students make connections and inferences.

- *What was the weather like in the story?*
- *Which season was it?*
- *How did Mike know it was snowing?*
- *Who lives next door to Mike?*
- *What are some things the friends might do in the snow?*

Day 1 picture

Follow Directions

Have students look at the picture. Then say:

Listen carefully and follow my directions.

- *What winter clothes did Mike wear to go out in the snow?* (coat, hat, boots, mittens) *Make an orange dot on Mike's coat. Make a black dot on his boots.*
- *Why did Mike want to go outside?* (to play in the snow) *Make a blue dot on some of the snow on the tree branches.*
- *Where was Mike's scarf?* (on the dog) *Make a red dot on the scarf. Make a brown dot on the dog.*

Have students color the picture according to the dots they made.

SKILLS:

Listening and Speaking
- Interpret illustrations
- Use new vocabulary
- Take turns speaking in a group
- Speak in complete sentences
- Relate new vocabulary to prior knowledge
- Respond appropriately to directions and questions

Comprehension
- Note details
- Recall details
- Respond to open-ended questions
- Make connections using illustrations, prior knowledge, and real-life experiences

Recalling the Story

Guide a discussion that helps students recall the Day 1 story. Reread the story if necessary. Say:

We listened to a story about Mike. It was winter.

- *What did Mike want to do when he saw the snow?*
- *Does it ever snow where you live? Do you like the snow? Why or why not?*

Distribute the Day 2 activity. Then say:

Listen carefully and follow my directions.

- *What do you see in box 1?* (It is snowing outside.) *Did that happen in the story? Color the happy face for* **yes** *or the sad face for* **no.** (yes)
- *What do you see in box 2?* (Mike is watching TV.) *Did that happen in the story? Color the happy face for* **yes** *or the sad face for* **no.** (no) *What did Mike do instead of watching TV?* (He went outside to play with his friend Jesse.)
- *What do you see in box 3?* (Mike is putting on his coat.) *Did that happen in the story? Color the happy face for* **yes** *or the sad face for* **no.** (yes)
- *What do you see in box 4?* (The dog has Mike's mitten.) *Did that happen in the story? Color the happy face for* **yes** *or the sad face for* **no.** (no)

Day 2 activity

SKILLS:

Listening and Speaking
- Use new vocabulary
- Follow directions
- Use language to show reasoning
- Describe people, places, things, locations, and actions
- Respond appropriately to directions and questions

Comprehension
- Note details
- Recall details
- Compare and contrast

Motor Skills
- Develop small muscle coordination

Same and Different

Reread the Day 1 story if necessary. Say:

Our story was about a boy named Mike. He wanted to play outside in the snow.

- *What winter clothes did Mike put on?*
- *What was missing?*

Distribute the Day 3 activity. Then say:

Listen carefully and follow my directions.

- *What do you see in row 1?* (two scarves) *How are the scarves different?* (One has stripes.) *Make the scarves look the same. Draw stripes on the plain scarf.*

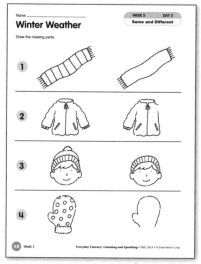

Day 3 activity

- *What do you see in row 2?* (coats) *How are the coats different?* (One is missing a sleeve.) *Draw the missing sleeve on the coat.*
- *What do you see in row 3?* (boys wearing hats) *How are the hats different?* (One is bigger.) *Make the hats look the same.*
- *What do you see in row 4?* (mittens) *How are the mittens different?* (the bottom, the polka dots) *Make the mittens look the same.*

Day 4

SKILLS:

Listening and Speaking
- Describe people, places, things, locations, and actions
- Respond appropriately to directions and questions
- Use new vocabulary
- Follow directions
- Interpret illustrations

Comprehension
- Compare and contrast
- Note details
- Recall details
- Make connections using illustrations, prior knowledge, and real-life experiences

Identifying Seasons

Reread the Day 1 story if necessary. Say:

Our story was about playing outside in winter.

- *What did Mike ask his mom if he could do?*
- *What did Mike wear to play outside?*

Distribute the Day 4 activity. Then say:

Listen carefully and follow my directions.

- *Look at row 1. Which picture shows a boy dressed for winter?* (the first picture) *What is he wearing?* (hat, coat, boots) *Circle the first picture.*
- *Look at row 2. Which picture shows a boy playing outside in winter?* (the middle picture) *What is he doing?* (making a snowman) *Circle the middle picture.*
- *Look at row 3. Which picture shows how trees look in winter?* (the last picture) *How do you know it is winter?* (There is snow. There are no leaves on the tree.) *Circle the last picture.*

Have students color the pictures they circled.

Day 4 activity

Day 5

SKILLS:

Listening and Speaking
- Use new vocabulary
- Speak in complete sentences
- Describe ideas, feelings, and experiences
- Develop auditory memory
- Recite short poems, rhymes, and songs

Comprehension
- Respond to open-ended questions

Home–School Connection p. 50
Spanish version available (see p. 2)

Circle Activity

Have students sit in a circle on the rug. Then connect the story to students' lives by asking:

- *Have you ever played in the snow?*
- *What would you like to do in the snow?*

Introduce the chant below by reading the first line and having the class echo you. Then model completing the sentence frame. Go around the circle, with the class chanting the first line together and each student taking a turn completing the sentence frame.

Chant together: *What do you play on a cold winter day?*

First student: *I _____ on a cold winter day.*

Chant together: *What do you play on a cold winter day?*

Second student: *I _____ on a cold winter day.*

Extend the Activity

Have students draw pictures of what they like to do on cold winter days. Then have them add "snow" by gluing cotton balls on their pictures.

Name _____

Winter Weather

Name _____

Winter Weather

Did it happen in the story?

1. ☺ yes   ☹ no

2. ☺ yes   ☹ no

3. ☺ yes   ☹ no

4. ☺ yes   ☹ no

Name _____

Winter Weather

Draw the missing parts.

1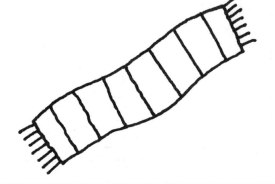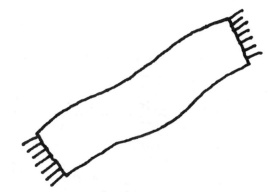

2

3

4

Everyday Literacy: Listening and Speaking • EMC 2415 • © Evan-Moor Corp.

Name _____

Winter Weather

Listen and follow the directions.

Name _____

What I Learned

To Parents

This week, your child listened to the story "Winter Weather." In the story, Mike saw the snow outside and asked his mom if he could play with Jesse next door. He put on a coat, hat, boots, and mittens. He couldn't find his scarf because his dog was wearing it.

What to Do

Have your child tell you what is happening in the picture. Ask questions such as: *Which season is it? What is Mike wearing to keep warm in winter? What couldn't he find to wear? What do you think he will do in the snow?* Encourage your child to use the vocabulary words in the box. Then have him or her color the picture.

Concept
Winter is a season.

Oral Vocabulary

boots	mittens
coat	scarf
hat	snow
jacket	winter

What to Do Next

Place several pieces of your child's clothing on a bed. Ask your child which clothes he or she wears during each season and why. Then read aloud a story about winter, such as *The Snowy Day* by Ezra Jack Keats.

Everyday Literacy: Listening and Speaking • EMC 2415 • © Evan-Moor Corp.

Spring Is Here

Oral Vocabulary

Naming words: nest, raincoat, spring
Action word: rain
Describing words: blue, green, purple, yellow

Day 1

SKILLS:

**Listening and
Speaking**
• Speak audibly
• Speak in complete
sentences
• Take turns speaking
in a group
• Follow directions
• Use new vocabulary
• Relate new
vocabulary to prior
knowledge
• Respond
appropriately to
directions and
questions
• Interpret illustrations

Comprehension
• Make inferences and
draw conclusions
• Note details
• Recall details
• Make connections
using illustrations,
prior knowledge, and
real-life experiences

Listening to the Story

Distribute the Day 1 picture to each student. Say: *There are four seasons.
Each one is different. Spring is a season.* Then read aloud the story below. Ask
students to listen carefully as you read.

---

*Spring is here! It rains a lot during spring, and today is a rainy
day. My dad and I love the rain. We put on our yellow raincoats and
go outside. Everywhere we look, we see the color green. The hills are
covered in green grass, and little green leaves are growing on the
trees. Purple flowers on green stems are growing all around.*

"Look, Max!" says Dad. "There are two baby bluebirds in a nest!"
"I see them!" I say. "Spring is my favorite season."

Making Inferences

Guide students in looking at the picture and
discussing the story. Use the questions below
to help students make connections and inferences.

Day 1 picture

• *Why are Max and his dad wearing
raincoats?*
• *What color does Max see everywhere?*
• *What is in the nest?*
• *Which season does Max like best?*

Following Directions

Have students look at the picture. Then say:

Listen carefully and follow my directions.

• *Where can you see new spring leaves?* (on the tree) *What else is in the
tree?* (a nest with baby birds) *Make a brown dot on the nest. Make
a blue dot on each baby bird.*

• *What are Max and his dad wearing?* (raincoats) *Why?* (because it is raining)
Make a yellow dot on the raincoats. Then draw some raindrops in the sky.

• *What grows green in spring?* (grass, leaves, stems) *Make a green dot
on the grass, a leaf, and a flower stem.*

Have students color the picture according to the dots they made.

SKILLS:

Listening and Speaking
- Respond appropriately to questions and directions
- Use new vocabulary
- Interpret illustrations
- Speak in complete sentences
- Speak audibly
- Identify and sort common words into basic categories
- Identify a wide variety of objects

Comprehension
- Categorize and classify
- Recall details

Categorizing

Guide a discussion that helps students recall the Day 1 story. Reread the story if necessary. Say:

We listened to a story about Max and his dad. They go for a walk one rainy spring day.

- *What do Max and his dad wear?*
- *What do they see in a tree?*

Distribute the Day 2 activity. Then say:

Listen carefully and follow my directions.

- *Look at row 1. I'll name the pictures:* **leaves, raincoat, hill**. *Which things are green in the story?* (leaves, hill) *Color them green.*

- *Look at row 2. Let's name these things together:* **raincoat, hill, birds**. *What is yellow in the story?* (raincoat) *Color it yellow.*

- *Look at row 3. Let's name these things together:* **leaves, birds, raincoat**. *Which things are blue in the story?* (birds) *Color them blue.*

- *Look at row 4. Let's name these things together:* **hill, flower, tree**. *What is purple in the story?* (flower) *Color it purple.*

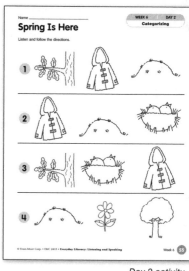

Day 2 activity

SKILLS:

Listening and Speaking
- Follow directions
- Use new vocabulary
- Listen critically to interpret and evaluate
- Respond appropriately to directions and questions
- Speak audibly

Comprehension
- Recall details

Phonological Awareness
- Blend the sounds of an onset/rime of a spoken word

Blending Onsets and Rimes

Reread the Day 1 story if necessary. Say:

Our story is about Max and his dad going outside on a rainy spring day.

- *What new things grow in spring?*

Distribute the Day 3 activity. Then say:

Listen carefully and follow my directions. I will say two word parts and then say the whole word.

- *Let's practice. Listen:* **M•ax**. *The word is* **Max**.

- *Now it's your turn. Look at box 1. Listen while I say two word parts:* **b•ird**. *What is the word?* (**bird**) *Circle the bird.*

- *Look at box 2. Listen while I say two word parts:* **n•est**. *What is the word?* (**nest**) *Circle the nest.*

- *Look at box 3. Listen while I say two word parts:* **r•ain**. *What is the word?* (**rain**) *Circle the raindrops.*

- *Look at box 4. Listen while I say two word parts:* **l•eaf**. *What is the word?* (**leaf**) *Circle the leaf.*

Day 3 activity

SKILLS:

Listening and Speaking
• Use new vocabulary
• Follow directions
• Identify a wide variety of objects
• Speak in complete sentences
• Interpret illustrations

Comprehension
• Recall details
• Make connections using illustrations

Motor Skills
• Develop small muscle coordination

Finishing a Picture

Reread the Day 1 story if necessary. Say:

This week, our story is about a spring day.

> • *What colors do Max and his dad see?*
> • *What is Max's favorite season?*

Distribute the Day 4 activity and crayons. Say:

Listen carefully and follow my directions to finish the picture.

> • *What does the picture show?* (baby birds in a nest)
> • *It often rains in spring. The rain is falling on the birds. Draw 5 raindrops falling on the birds.*
> • *The mother bird used some flowers to build her nest. Draw 2 purple flowers on the nest.*
> • *Leaves pop out on trees in spring. Draw 3 leaves on the tree branch.*
> • *Look below the picture. Put your finger on the first letter, **s**. The letters make a word. The word is **spring**. Move your finger under the letters and say the word **spring**.*

Day 4 activity

SKILLS:

Listening and Speaking
• Use new vocabulary
• Recite short poems, rhymes, and songs
• Follow directions
• Develop auditory memory

Comprehension
• Recall details

Circle Activity

Have students sit in a circle on the rug. Then connect the story to students' lives by asking:

> • *What is the weather like in the story?*
> • *What is the weather like here during spring?*
> • *What changes do we see outside during spring?*

Teach this song, sung to the tune of "Frere Jacques."

> *In the springtime, in the springtime, raindrops fall, raindrops fall.*
> *Springtime is a fine time. Springtime is a fine time.*
> *Raindrops fall. Raindrops fall.*
>
> *In the springtime, in the springtime, grass is green, grass is green.*
> *Springtime is a fine time. Springtime is a fine time.*
> *Grass is green. Grass is green.*

Extend the Activity

Have students suggest other things to sing about that happen in spring (e.g., "...leaves are new." or "...baby birds chirp.").

Name _____

Spring Is Here

Name _____

Spring Is Here

Listen and follow the directions.

1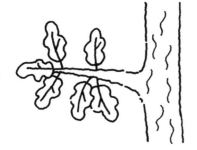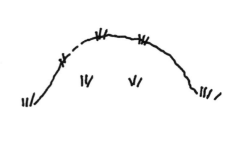

2

3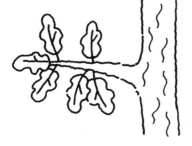

4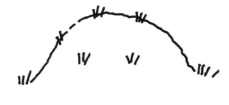

Name _____

Spring Is Here

Listen and follow the directions.

Everyday Literacy: Listening and Speaking • EMC 2415 • © Evan-Moor Corp.

Name _____

Spring Is Here

Listen and draw.

spring

Name _____

What I Learned

To Parents
This week, your child listened to the story "Spring Is Here." In the story, Max and his dad put on their raincoats and take a springtime walk outside in the rain. They see hills covered in green grass and green leaves on the trees. They also see some purple flowers growing and baby bluebirds in a nest. Max says that spring is his favorite season.

Concept
Spring is a season.

Oral Vocabulary

blue	rain
green	raincoat
nest	spring
purple	yellow

What to Do
Have your child tell you what is happening in the picture. Ask questions such as: *What season is it? What is the weather like? What are Max and his dad wearing? What do they see outside? What color are the leaves and grass? What color are the birds?* Encourage your child to use the vocabulary words in the box. Then have him or her color the picture.

What to Do Next
Make a rain painting with your child. Provide him or her with a sturdy, uncoated (not shiny) paper plate. Squeeze out drops of food coloring on the plate. Set the plate outside in a gentle rain and watch the results together. If it's not raining, use a lawn sprinkler or a spray bottle to spray the plate with water.

Everyday Literacy: Listening and Speaking • EMC 2415 • © Evan-Moor Corp.

WEEK 7

Concept
Summer is a season.

A Summer Day

Oral Vocabulary

Naming words: ladybug, snail, summer, worm
Action words: crawl, creep, squirm, wiggle

Day 1

SKILLS:

Listening and Speaking
• Respond appropriately to directions and questions
• Speak in complete sentences
• Take turns speaking in a group
• Follow directions
• Use new vocabulary
• Relate new vocabulary to prior knowledge
• Identify a wide variety of objects
• Speak audibly
• Listen for different purposes

Comprehension
• Make inferences and draw conclusions
• Note details
• Recall details

Listening to the Story

Distribute the Day 1 picture to each student. Say: *There are four seasons. Each one is different. Summer is a season.* Then read aloud the story below. Ask students to listen carefully as you read.

What do you like to do in summer? I like to sit in the garden and watch things creep and crawl. This morning, I saw three ladybugs fly around and land on the fence. Then I saw two snails crawl under a leaf to hide from me. The best part was the worm that crawled across my hand. It wiggled and squirmed to find its way back to the cool dirt. My garden is alive with interesting creatures.

Making Inferences

Guide students in looking at the picture and discussing the story. Use the questions below to help students make connections and inferences.

• *Which season was it?*
• *What creatures lived in the garden?*

Following Directions

Have students look at the picture. Then say:
Listen carefully and follow my directions.

• *What does the girl in the story like to do on a summer day?* (sit in the garden and watch things creep and crawl) *What crawled across her hand?* (a worm) *Make an orange dot on the girl's shirt. Draw a pink circle around the worm.*

• *You can see many creatures in summer. What other creatures did the girl watch?* (three ladybugs and two snails) *What did the ladybugs do?* (flew around and landed on the fence) *What did the snails do?* (crawled under a leaf to hide) *Draw a red circle around each ladybug. Draw a brown circle around each snail.*

• *What do you see growing in the garden?* (flowers) *What is your favorite color of flower? Make that color dot on each flower.*

Have students color the picture according to the dots they made.

Day 1 picture

Name _____
A Summer Day
WEEK 7   DAY 1
Following Directions

62 Week 7   *Everyday Literacy: Listening and Speaking* • EMC 2415 • © Evan-Moor Corp.

SKILLS:

Listening and Speaking
• Use new vocabulary
• Follow directions
• Interpret illustrations
• Respond appropriately to directions and questions
• Speak in complete sentences
• Identify a wide variety of objects

Comprehension
• Recall details

Recalling the Story

Guide a discussion that helps students recall the Day 1 story. Reread the story if necessary. Say:

We listened to a story about a girl in a garden.

> • *Which season was it?*
>
> • *What landed on the fence?*
>
> • *What did the girl think was the best part of her day?*

Distribute the Day 2 activity. Then say:

Listen carefully and follow my directions.

> • *What do you see in box 1?* (a worm crawling across a girl's hand) *Did a worm crawl across a girl's hand in the story? Color the happy face for* **yes** *or the sad face for* **no***.* (yes)
>
> • *What do you see in box 2?* (a girl reading a book) *Did a girl read a book in the story? Color the happy face for* **yes** *or the sad face for* **no***.* (no)
>
> • *What do you see in box 3?* (a snail crawling on a fence) *Did a snail crawl on the fence in the story? Color the happy face for* **yes** *or the sad face for* **no***.* (no)
>
> • *What do you see in box 4?* (ladybugs on a fence) *How many ladybugs are there?* (three) *Did three ladybugs land on a fence in the story? Color the happy face for* **yes** *or the sad face for* **no***.* (yes)

Day 2 activity

SKILLS:

Listening and Speaking
• Follow directions
• Use new vocabulary
• Relate new vocabulary to prior knowledge

Comprehension
• Make inferences and draw conclusions
• Make connections using illustrations and prior knowledge
• Respond to open-ended questions
• Recall details

Motor Skills
• Develop small muscle coordination

Using Small Motor Skills

Reread the Day 1 story if necessary. Say:

Our story was about a summer day. A girl sat outside in the garden.

> • *What did the girl watch?*
>
> • *What creatures hid under a leaf?*
>
> • *What might you see on summer days?*

Distribute the Day 3 activity and crayons. Say:

Let's finish the picture on this page.

> • *Put your crayon on the star. Trace the line around and around. See if you can do it without picking up your crayon.*
>
> • *What did you make?* (a snail's shell)
>
> • *Where do you think the snail lives?* (in a garden)
>
> • *Draw a flower on each stem to make the snail's garden.*
>
> • *Have you ever seen a real snail? Where did you see it?* (Answers vary.)

Have students color the picture.

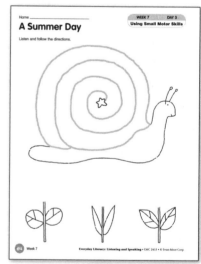

Day 3 activity

SKILLS:

Listening and Speaking
- Interpret illustrations
- Listen for different purposes
- Respond appropriately to directions and questions
- Follow directions
- Use new vocabulary
- Listen critically to interpret and evaluate

Comprehension
- Recall details
- Respond to open-ended questions

Phonological Awareness
- Identify examples of alliteration in spoken language
- Identify common beginning consonant sounds in spoken words

Listening for Beginning Sounds

Reread the Day 1 story if necessary. Say:

This week, our story was about a girl who sat in a garden on a summer day.

- *What was alive in the garden?*

Distribute the Day 4 activity. Then say:

Day 4 activity

- *Look at the girl in the first box. Listen while I read a sentence. Listen carefully for the beginning sound in each word:* **Lisa likes ladybugs**. *What sound did you hear at the beginning of each word?* (**/l/**) *Let's say the sentence together. I'll hold up a finger every time we say /l/:* **Lisa likes ladybugs**. *How many times did you hear the /l/ sound?* (three) *Circle the* **3**.

- *Look at the boy sitting on the beach. Listen:* **Hand Hank his hat**. *What sound did you hear at the beginning of each word?* (**/h/**) *Let's say the sentence together. I'll hold up a finger every time we say /h/:* **Hand Hank his hat**. *How many times did you hear /h/?* (four) *Circle the* **4**.

- *Look at the boy watching worms. Listen:* **William watches worms wiggle**. *What sound did you hear at the beginning of each word?* (**/w/**) *Let's say the sentence together. I'll hold up a finger every time we say /w/:* **William watches worms wiggle**. *How many times did you hear /w/?* (four) *Circle the* **4**.

- *Look at the girl watching snails. Listen:* **Sarah saw six snails**. *What sound did you hear at the beginning of each word?* (**/s/**) *Let's say the sentence together. I'll hold up a finger every time we say /s/:* **Sarah saw six snails**. *How many times did you hear /s/?* (four) *Circle the* **4**.

SKILLS:

Listening and Speaking
- Develop auditory memory
- Take turns speaking in a group
- Speak in complete sentences
- Recite short poems, rhymes, and songs

Comprehension
- Recall details

Circle Activity

Have students sit in a circle on the rug. Then connect the story to students' lives by asking:

- *What is the weather like here during summer?*
- *Do you have a garden or yard? What creatures might you see in it?*

Introduce the chant below by reading the first line and having the class echo you. Then model completing the sentence frame. Go around the circle, with the class chanting the first line together and each student taking a turn completing the sentence frame.

Chant together: *What would you see on a summer day?*

Student 1: *I would see _____ on a summer day.*

Home–School Connection p. 66
Spanish version available (see p. 2)

Extend the Activity

Have students draw pictures of creatures they have seen in the garden during summer.

Name _____

A Summer Day

Everyday Literacy: Listening and Speaking • EMC 2415 • © Evan-Moor Corp.

Name _____

A Summer Day

Did it happen in the story?

1

 yes   no

2

yes    no

3

yes   no

4

yes    no

Name _____

A Summer Day

Listen and follow the directions.

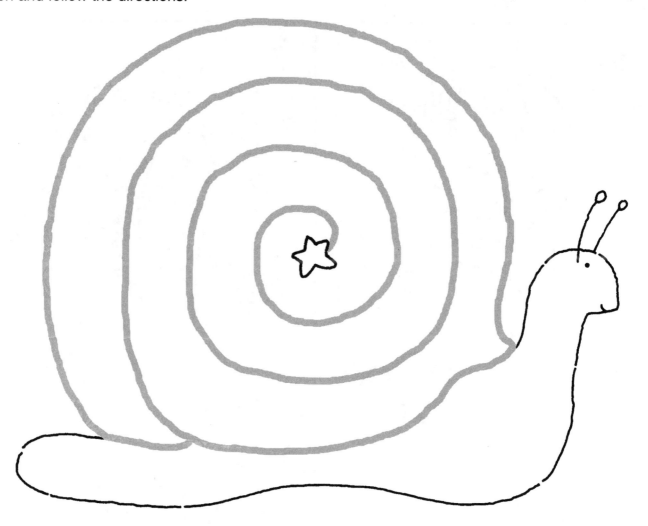

 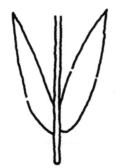 

Everyday Literacy: Listening and Speaking • EMC 2415 • © Evan-Moor Corp.

Name _____

A Summer Day

Listen and follow the directions.

3   4   5

3   4   5

3   4   5

3   4   5

Name _____

What I Learned

To Parents

This week, your child listened to the story "A Summer Day." In the story, a girl likes to sit in her garden in the summer. One morning, she watched ladybugs land on the fence and snails crawl under a leaf. Best of all, a worm crawled across her hand.

What to Do

Have your child tell you what is happening in the picture. Ask questions such as: *What creatures are creeping and crawling in the garden? How many ladybugs do you see? How many snails are there? What is the worm doing? What season is it?* Encourage your child to use the vocabulary words in the box. Then have him or her color the picture.

Concept
Summer is a season.

Oral Vocabulary

crawl	squirm
creep	summer
ladybug	wiggle
snail	worm

What to Do Next

Make a collage of creatures that creep and crawl in summer. Look through magazines or search the Internet with your child. Cut out or print pictures of creatures such as ladybugs, snails, worms, beetles, flies, mosquitoes, dragonflies, and bees. Help your child glue the pictures on a piece of paper.

Everyday Literacy: Listening and Speaking • EMC 2415 • © Evan-Moor Corp.

Concept

Caring for plants helps them grow.

In the Garden

Oral Vocabulary

Naming words: hose, tomato, weeds

Action words: pick, plant, pull, water

Day 1

SKILLS:

Listening and Speaking
- Respond appropriately to directions and questions
- Speak in complete sentences
- Take turns speaking in a group
- Use language to show reasoning
- Follow directions
- Use new vocabulary
- Relate new vocabulary to prior knowledge
- Speak audibly
- Describe people, places, things, locations, and actions

Comprehension
- Make inferences and draw conclusions
- Note details
- Recall details
- Make connections using illustrations, prior knowledge, and real-life experiences
- Respond to open-ended questions

Listening to the Story

Distribute the Day 1 picture to each student. Then read aloud the story below. Ask students to listen carefully as you read.

Grandpa taught me how to work in the garden. We planted little tomato plants. Then I helped Grandpa water the garden. I used a hose to water each plant. Every week, we pulled the weeds. Our tomato plants grew and grew.

Now we have a lot of big, red tomatoes. We picked a basket full. Then Grandpa showed me how to make the world's best tomato sandwiches. We ate them for lunch. Yum!

Making Inferences

Guide students in looking at the picture and discussing the story. Use the questions below to help students make connections and inferences.

- *Where do tomatoes come from?*
- *What did the boy do to take care of the tomato plants?*

Following Directions

Have students look at the picture. Then say:

Listen carefully and follow my directions.

Day 1 picture

- *Who taught the boy how to grow tomatoes?* (his grandpa) *What else did Grandpa teach him to do?* (how to make the world's best tomato sandwiches) *Make a blue dot on Grandpa's shirt. Make a brown dot on his hat.*

- *Let's think of words that tell what a tomato looks and feels like* (**big**, **red**, **squishy**, **yummy**) *Where are the tomatoes growing?* (on the plants) *Have you ever grown tomatoes? Have you grown anything else?* (Answers vary.) *Make red dots on some of the tomatoes.*

- *What did the boy use to water the plants?* (a hose) *Make an orange dot on the boy's shirt. Make a green dot on the hose.*

Have students color the picture according to the dots they made.

Day 2

SKILLS:

Listening and Speaking
- Speak in complete sentences
- Respond appropriately to directions and questions
- Use new vocabulary
- Interpret illustrations
- Follow directions

Comprehension
- Make connections using illustrations, prior knowledge, and real-life experiences
- Note details
- Recall details

Recalling the Story

Guide a discussion that helps students recall the Day 1 story. Reread the story if necessary. Say:

Out story was about a boy and his grandpa.

- *What did the boy and his grandpa do?*

Distribute the Day 2 activity. Then say:

Listen carefully and follow my directions.

- *What do you see in box 1?* (a boy planting a tomato plant) *Did the boy and his grandpa plant tomato plants? Color the happy face for* **yes** *or the sad face for* **no**. (yes)

- *What do you see in box 2?* (a man on a tractor) *Did the boy and his grandpa use a tractor? Color the happy face for* **yes** *or the sad face for* **no**. (no)

- *What do you see in box 3?* (a lady and a boy buying tomatoes) *Did the boy in the story buy tomatoes at the grocery store? Color the happy face for* **yes** *or the sad face for* **no**. (no) *Have you ever bought tomatoes at the store?* (Answers vary.)

- *What do you see in box 4?* (a man and a boy eating tomato sandwiches) *Did the boy and his grandpa eat tomato sandwiches? Color the happy face for* **yes** *or the sad face for* **no**. (yes)

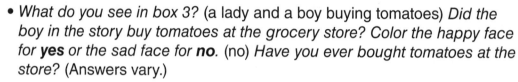

Day 2 activity

Day 3

SKILLS:

Listening and Speaking
- Speak in complete sentences
- Use new vocabulary
- Interpret illustrations
- Follow directions
- Describe people, places, things, locations, and actions
- Respond appropriately to directions and questions

Comprehension
- Identify a sequence of events
- Recall details
- Make connections using illustrations and prior knowledge

Motor Skills
- Develop small muscle coordination

Sequencing

Reread the Day 1 story if necessary. Say:

In our story, the boy helped in the garden.

- *What did the boy learn to do?*

Distribute the Day 3 activity. Then say:

Listen carefully and follow my directions.

- *Find the star. Think about how a tomato plant grows. Which picture in that row shows what happens first?* (planting a little plant) *Trace the* **1** *below the picture. What happens next?* (watering the plant) *Trace the* **2** *below the picture. What happens last?* (growing into a big plant) *Trace the* **3** *below the picture.*

Day 3 activity

- *Find the triangle. Think about what you have to do to eat a tomato. Which picture in that row shows what happens first?* (picking) *Write* **1** *below the picture. What happens next?* (washing) *Write* **2** *below the picture. What happens last?* (slicing) *Write* **3** *below the picture.*

- *Find the square. Think about making a tomato sandwich. What happens first?* (getting bread and a tomato) *Write* **1** *below the picture. What happens next?* (making a sandwich) *Write* **2** *below the picture. What happens last?* (eating the sandwich) *Write* **3** *below the picture.*

Day 4

SKILLS:

Listening and Speaking
• Listen critically to interpret and evaluate
• Follow directions
• Listen for different purposes
• Identify a wide variety of objects

Comprehension
• Recall details

Phonological Awareness
• Identify common beginning consonant sounds in spoken words

Listening for Beginning Sounds

Reread the Day 1 story if necessary. Say:

Our story was about growing tomatoes.

• *What work did the boy do in the garden?*

• *What did the boy and his grandpa do after they picked tomatoes?*

Distribute the Day 4 activity. Then say:

Listen carefully and follow my directions.

Day 4 activity

• *Point to the tomato. Listen for the sound at the beginning of* **tomato**: */t/. Which picture in that row also begins with the /t/ sound: /t/* **table** *or /r/* **rake***? (table) Circle the table.*

• *Point to the sandwich. Listen for the sound at the beginning of* **sandwich**: */s/. Which picture in that row also begins with /s/: /b/* **basket** *or /s/* **sun***? (sun) Circle the sun.*

• *Point to the hose. Listen for the sound at the beginning of* **hose**: */h/. Which picture in that row also begins with /h/: /b/* **boy** *or /h/* **hat***? (hat) Circle the hat.*

• *Point to the garden. Listen for the sound at the beginning of* **garden**: */g/. Which picture in that row also begins with /g/: /g/* **gate** *or /r/* **rabbit***? (gate) Circle the gate.*

Day 5

SKILLS:

Listening and Speaking
• Use new vocabulary
• Recite short poems, rhymes, and songs
• Follow directions
• Develop auditory memory

Comprehension
• Recall details

Circle Activity

Have students sit in a circle on the rug. Then review the concepts and vocabulary they practiced this week. Ask:

• *How did the boy and his grandpa take care of the tomato plants?*

• *What did they do when the tomatoes were big and red?*

Teach this song, sung to the tune of "Row, Row, Row Your Boat." Invite students to suggest actions for each verse.

Plant, plant, plant some plants, in my little garden.
I take care of the plants, in my little garden

Water, water, water the plants in my little garden. I take care…
Pull, pull, pull the weeds in my little garden. I take care…
Pick, pick, pick tomatoes, in my little garden. I take care…
Eat, eat, eat tomatoes, from my little garden. I take care…

Home–School Connection p. 74
Spanish version available (see p. 2)

Extend the Activity

Have students suggest other garden vegetables to substitute in the last two verses (e.g., "Pick, pick, pick the beans…").

Name _____

In the Garden

Everyday Literacy: Listening and Speaking • EMC 2415 • © Evan-Moor Corp.

Name _____

In the Garden

Did it happen in the story?

1. 😊 yes 😞 no

2. 😊 yes 😞 no

3. 😊 yes 😞 no

4. 😊 yes 😞 no

Name _____

In the Garden

Write **1**, **2**, or **3** to show the order.

⭐   3   ___ | ___   2   ___

___   ___   ___

___   ___   ___

Name _____

In the Garden

Listen for the beginning sound.

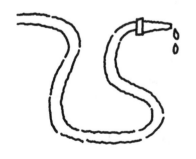  

Name _____

What I Learned

To Parents
This week, your child listened to the story "In the Garden." In the story, a boy and his grandpa planted little tomato plants. The boy helped care for the plants by watering them and pulling the weeds. When the tomatoes were big and red, they picked some. Then the grandpa showed the boy how to make the world's best tomato sandwiches.

Concept
Caring for plants helps them grow.

Oral Vocabulary

hose	tomato
pick	water
plant	weeds
pull	

What to Do
Have your child tell you what is happening in the picture. Ask your child questions such as: *Where did the boy and his grandpa plant the tomato plants? What did they do to make the plants grow? What did they do when the tomatoes were big and red? What did the grandpa show the boy how to make?* Encourage your child to use the vocabulary words in the box. Then have him or her color the picture.

What to Do Next
Help your child plant seeds in cups of soil to make a window sill garden. Tomato, radish, and lettuce seeds will sprout in about a week. As the seeds grow, have your child keep the soil moist.

Concept

Insects have six legs; spiders have eight.

Insects and Spiders

Oral Vocabulary

Naming words: bug, grasshopper, insect, spider
Describing words: eight, six

Day 1

SKILLS:

Listening and Speaking
• Understand and use words for categories
• Respond appropriately to directions and questions
• Speak in complete sentences
• Speak audibly
• Take turns speaking in a group
• Follow directions
• Use new vocabulary
• Relate new vocabulary to prior knowledge
• Interpret illustrations
• Identify a wide variety of objects

Comprehension
• Note details
• Recall details
• Compare and contrast
• Categorize and classify
• Make inferences and draw conclusions

Listening to the Story

Distribute the Day 1 picture to each student. Then read aloud the story below. Ask students to listen carefully as you read.

I like to look for bugs in my backyard. Did you know that most bugs are really insects or spiders? Today, I learned the difference between an insect and a spider. An insect has six legs. A spider has eight legs. Now I know how to tell the difference when I see them in the garden. I found a grasshopper and counted its legs. It's an insect!

Making Inferences

Guide students in looking at the picture and discussing the story. Use the questions below to help students make connections and inferences.

• *What are other names for bugs?*
• *How are insects and spiders different?*
• *How many legs does a grasshopper have?*

Following Directions

Have students look at the picture. Then say:

Listen carefully and follow my directions.

Day 1 picture

• *What is the girl looking at?* (bugs in her backyard) *How many legs does a spider have?* (eight) *Draw a brown circle around the spider. Make a red dot on the girl's shirt.*

• *What insect does the girl see on a leaf?* (a grasshopper) *How many legs does it have?* (six) *Draw a green circle around the grasshopper. Make a green dot on a leaf.*

• *Can you find the ladybug? Where is it?* (on the fence) *Can you find the butterfly? Where is it?* (in the air) *Draw a red circle around the ladybug. Draw a blue circle around the butterfly.*

• *Butterflies and ladybugs have six legs. Are they insects or spiders?* (insects) *Tell me how many insects are in the picture.* (three) *How many spiders are in the picture?* (one)

Have students color the picture.

SKILLS:

Listening and Speaking
• Use new vocabulary
• Follow directions
• Speak in complete sentences
• Respond appropriately to directions and questions

Comprehension
• Compare and contrast
• Note details
• Recall details
• Categorize and classify

Motor Skills
• Develop small muscle coordination

Using Small Motor Skills

Guide a discussion that helps students recall the Day 1 story. Reread the story if necessary. Say:

Our story is about a girl who likes to look for bugs in her backyard.

* *What are other names for bugs?*
* *How are insects and spiders different?*

Distribute the Day 2 activity. Say:

Listen carefully and follow my directions.

* *Find the grasshopper. How many legs does it have?* (six) *Is it an insect?* (yes) *How do you know?* (It has six legs.) *Trace the grasshopper's six legs. Then trace the number* **6**.

* *Find the spider. How many legs does it have?* (eight) *Trace the spider's eight legs. Then trace the number* **8**. *How can you tell a spider from an insect?* (count its legs)

Have students color the grasshopper and spider.

Day 2 activity

SKILLS:

Listening and Speaking
• Identify a wide variety of objects
• Use new vocabulary
• Follow directions
• Use language to show reasoning
• Respond appropriately to directions and questions

Comprehension
• Make inferences and draw conclusions
• Categorize and classify
• Note details
• Recall details

Categorizing

Reread the Day 1 story if necessary. Say:

Our story is about a girl who likes to look for insects and spiders in her backyard.

* *What did she learn about insects?*
* *What did she learn about spiders?*

Distribute the Day 3 activity. Then say:

Listen carefully and follow my directions.

* *Put your finger on the grasshopper at the top of the page. The grasshopper is hungry!*

* *Look at each box on the page. What do you see?* (insects **or** grasshopper, ladybug, butterfly, bee) *Make a green dot on each grasshopper you see in a box.*

* *Now color only the boxes that have a green dot. You will make a path. The path goes to something a grasshopper likes to eat. Let's find out what it is.*

* *How many boxes did you color?* (six) *Where did the path go?* (to the leaf) *What does that mean?* (The grasshopper likes to eat leaves.)

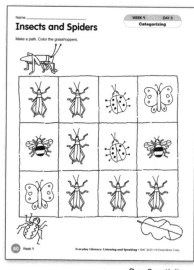

Day 3 activity

SKILLS:

Listening and Speaking
• Identify a wide variety of objects
• Follow directions
• Listen for different purposes
• Relate new vocabulary to prior knowledge
• Respond appropriately to directions and questions

Comprehension
• Recall details

Phonological Awareness
• Identify common beginning consonants in spoken words

Listening for Beginning Sounds

Reread the Day 1 story if necessary. Say:

We listened to a story about insects and spiders.

• *How many legs does a grasshopper have?*

• *How many legs does a spider have?*

Distribute the Day 4 activity. Then say:

Listen carefully and follow my directions.

• *Look at box 1. Name the pictures.* (**ladybug**, **leaf**) *Do you hear the same beginning sound in **ladybug** and **leaf**? Color the happy face for **yes** or the sad face for **no**.* (yes) *What sound did you hear?* (/l/)

• *Look at box 2. Name the pictures.* (**girl**, **six**) *Do you hear the same beginning sound in **girl** and **six**? Color the happy face for **yes** or the sad face for **no**.* (no)

• *Look at box 3. Name the pictures.* (**butterfly**, **bee**) *Do you hear the same beginning sound in **butterfly** and **bee**? Color the happy face for **yes** or the sad face for **no**.* (yes) *What sound did you hear?* (/b/)

• *Look at box 4. Name the pictures.* (**worm**, **web**) *Do you hear the same beginning sound in **worm** and **web**? Color the happy face for **yes** or the sad face for **no**.* (yes) *What sound did you hear?* (/w/)

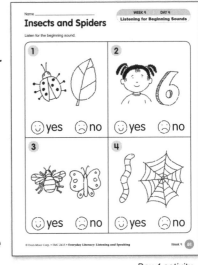

Day 4 activity

SKILLS:

Listening and Speaking
• Recite short poems, rhymes, and songs
• Follow directions
• Develop auditory memory

Comprehension
• Recall details
• Respond to open-ended questions

Motor Skills
• Develop large muscle coordination

Circle Activity

Have students sit in a circle on the rug. Then connect the story to students' lives by asking:

• *Where have you seen insects and spiders?*

• *Do you have a favorite insect? What is it? Why do you like it?*

Introduce and model the chant below. Then teach students how to play this game, which is similar to "Duck, Duck, Goose." Choose a student to be the "grasshopper." Have the grasshopper walk around the outside of the circle as the class recites the chant. On the word **me**, have the grasshopper tap another student. The student who is tapped should chase the grasshopper. If the grasshopper makes it back to the empty place in the circle before being tagged, the other student becomes the new grasshopper.

Chant together: *Float like a butterfly.*
Fly like a bee.
Hop like a grasshopper.
Try to catch me.

Extend the Activity

Make the game more challenging by specifying the type of movement for the players to use (e.g., run, hop, skip, baby steps, or giant steps).

Home–School Connection p. 82
Spanish version available (see p. 2)

Insects and Spiders

Name _____

Insects and Spiders

Listen and trace.

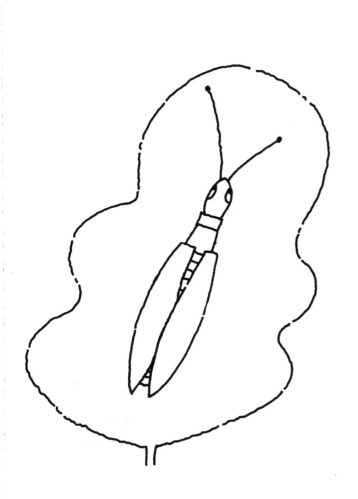

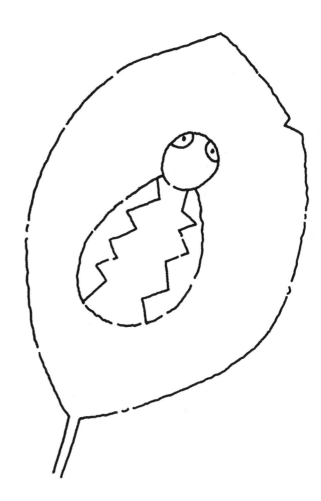

6
legs

8
legs

Insects and Spiders

Make a path. Color the grasshoppers.

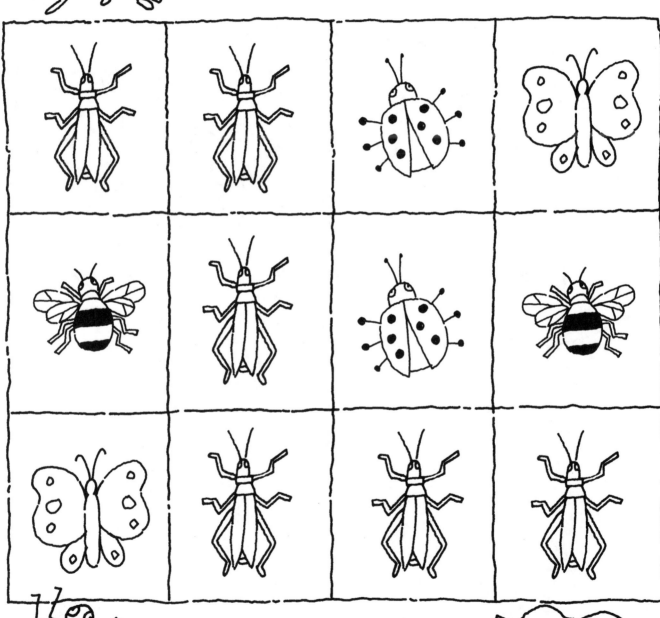

Everyday Literacy: Listening and Speaking • EMC 2415 • © Evan-Moor Corp.

Name _____

Insects and Spiders

Listen for the beginning sound.

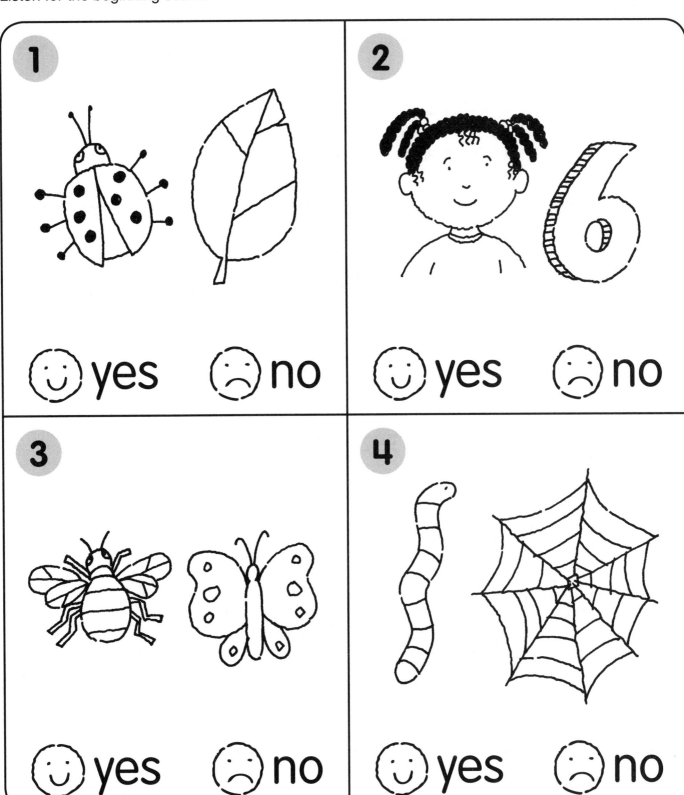

1

:) yes   :(no

2

:) yes   :(no

3

:) yes   :(no

4

:) yes   :(no

Name _____

What I Learned

To Parents

This week, your child listened to the story "Insects and Spiders." In the story, a girl learned that insects have six legs and spiders have eight. When she found a grasshopper, she counted its six legs and decided it's an insect.

What to Do

Have your child tell you what is happening in the picture. Have him or her name the insects and find the spider. Then ask how many legs each creature has. Encourage your child to use the vocabulary words in the box. Then have him or her color the picture.

Concept
Insects have six legs; spiders have eight.

Oral Vocabulary

bug	insect
eight	six
grasshopper	spider

What to Do Next

Go outside together and look for insects and spiders. Teach your child to look but not touch.

Everyday Literacy: Listening and Speaking • EMC 2415 • © Evan-Moor Corp.

Fire Safety

Oral Vocabulary

Naming words: firefighter, flames, safety
Action words: drop, roll, stop

Day 1

SKILLS:

Listening and Speaking
- Respond appropriately to directions and questions
- Speak in complete sentences
- Take turns speaking in a group
- Follow directions
- Use new vocabulary
- Relate new vocabulary to prior knowledge
- Retell a spoken message by summarizing or clarifying
- Describe ideas, feelings, and experiences
- Speak audibly
- Interpret illustrations

Comprehension
- Make inferences and draw conclusions
- Note details
- Recall details
- Respond to open-ended questions

Listening to the Story

Distribute the Day 1 picture to each student. Then read aloud the story below. Ask students to listen carefully as you read.

Firefighter Will and his partner Spot came to school. They taught us about fire safety. We learned what to do if our clothes catch fire. Never run! Stop right where you are. Drop to the ground. Roll to put out the flames. Firefighter Will taught Spot a trick. Can you guess what it is? Spot can stop, drop, and roll!

Making Inferences

Guide students in looking at the picture and discussing the story. Use the questions below to help students make connections and inferences.

- *What is happening in this picture?*
- *Who is Spot?*
- *If your clothes were to catch fire, what should you do?*
- *Why do you think Firefighter Will taught Spot how to stop, drop, and roll?*
- *What did Firefighter Will give each child to wear?*

Day 1 picture

Following Directions

Have students look at the picture. Then say:

Listen carefully and follow my directions.

- *Where are the children?* (at school) *Why did Firefighter Will come to school?* (to teach the students about fire safety) *How many firefighter hats do you see in the picture?* (five) *Make a red dot on each firefighter hat. Make a yellow dot on Firefighter Will.*
- *Whom did Firefighter Will bring with him to school?* (his dog Spot) *What trick did Spot show the students?* (how to stop, drop, and roll) *Have you ever met a firefighter? Tell me about it.* (Answers vary.) *Make a black dot on Spot's spots. Make a red dot on his collar.*

Have students color the picture according to the dots they made.

SKILLS:

Listening and Speaking
• Speak audibly
• Use new vocabulary
• Follow directions
• Interpret illustrations
• Respond appropriately to directions and questions

Comprehension
• Note details
• Recall details
• Make connections using illustrations and prior knowledge

Recalling the Story

Guide a discussion that helps students recall the Day 1 story. Reread the story if necessary. Say:

We listened to a story about fire safety.

> • *When should you stop, drop, and roll?*

Distribute the Day 2 activity. Then say:

Listen carefully and follow my directions.

> • *Look at row 1. Name the types of workers.* (police officer, firefighter, teacher) *In our story, who taught the students about fire safety?* (firefighter) *Draw a red line under the firefighter.*

> • *Look at row 2. Name the places.* (fire house, house, school) *In our story, where was Firefighter Will?* (school) *What was he doing there?* (teaching students about fire safety) *Draw a blue line under the school.*

> • *Look at row 3. Name the types of animals.* (cat, dog/Spot, mouse) *In our story, who showed the students a trick?* (dog/Spot) *What was the trick?* (Stop, drop, and roll.) *Draw a black line under Spot.*

> • *Look at row 4. Tell me what each child is doing.* (running, riding, rolling) *Which child shows what to do if your clothes catch fire?* (the child rolling) *Draw a green line under the child who is rolling on the ground.*

Day 2 activity

SKILLS:

Listening and Speaking
• Interpret illustrations
• Follow directions
• Use new vocabulary

Comprehension
• Make predictions
• Recall details

Phonological Awareness
• Recognize words that rhyme

Motor Skills
• Develop small muscle coordination

Using Small Motor Skills

Reread the Day 1 story if necessary. Say:

In our story, students learned about fire safety.

> • *What trick did Spot do for the students?*

Distribute the Day 3 activity. Then say:

Listen carefully and follow my directions.

> • *Find the stop sign. What do you think the word next to it says?* (**stop**) *Trace the word* **stop** *with your pencil.*

> • *Find the next picture. What is the child doing?* (kneeling on the ground) *What do you think the word says?* (**drop**) *Trace the word* **drop** *with your pencil.*

Day 3 activity

> • *Look at the last picture. What is the child doing?* (rolling on the ground) *What do you think the word says?* (**roll**) *Trace the word* **roll** *with your pencil.*

> • *Let's read the words together. Put your finger on each word as we read it:* **stop, drop, roll.** *Which of those words rhyme?* (**stop** and **drop**)

Listening for Consonant Sounds

Distribute the Day 4 activity. Say:

Listen carefully and follow my directions.

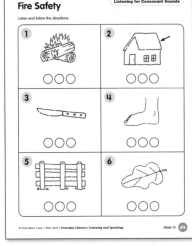

Day 4 activity

- *Look at box 1. Name the picture.* (**fire**) *Do you hear the /f/ sound at the beginning, middle, or end of **fire**?* (beginning) *Fill in the first circle.*

- *Look at box 2. Name the picture.* (**roof**) *Do you hear the /f/ sound at the beginning, middle, or end of **roof**?* (end) *Fill in the last circle.*

- *Look at box 3. Name the picture.* (**knife**) *Do you hear the /f/ sound at the beginning, middle, or end of **knife**?* (end) *Fill in the last circle.*

- *Look at box 4. Name the picture.* (**foot**) *Do you hear the /f/ sound at the beginning, middle, or end of **foot**?* (beginning) *Fill in the first circle.*

- *Look at box 5. Name the picture.* (**fence**) *Do you hear the /f/ sound at the beginning, middle, or end of **fence**?* (beginning) *Fill in the first circle.*

- *Look at box 6. Name the picture.* (**leaf**) *Do you hear the /f/ sound at the beginning, middle, or end of **leaf**?* (end) *Fill in the last circle.*

Circle Activity

Have students sit in a circle on the rug. Then review the concepts and vocabulary they practiced this week. Ask:

- *In the story, who came to school to teach fire safety?*

- *What did the students learn to do?*

Introduce and model the call-and-response chant below. When students are comfortable with the second verse, chant the first verse and have them answer with the second verse. Have students "stop, drop, and roll" each time they say those words.

Teacher: *What would you do?*
What would you do?
If your clothes should catch on fire,
What would you do?

Students: *Stop, drop, and roll.*
Stop, drop, and roll.
If my clothes should catch on fire,
Stop, drop, and roll.

Extend the Activity

Talk about other fire safety rules (e.g., Never touch matches, lighters, candles, or fireworks.).

Fire Safety

1. stop
2. drop
3. roll

Name _____

Fire Safety

Listen and follow the directions.

1

2

3

4

Name _____

Fire Safety

Listen and trace.

 stop

 drop

 roll

Everyday Literacy: Listening and Speaking • EMC 2415 • © Evan-Moor Corp.

Name _____

Fire Safety

Listen and follow the directions.

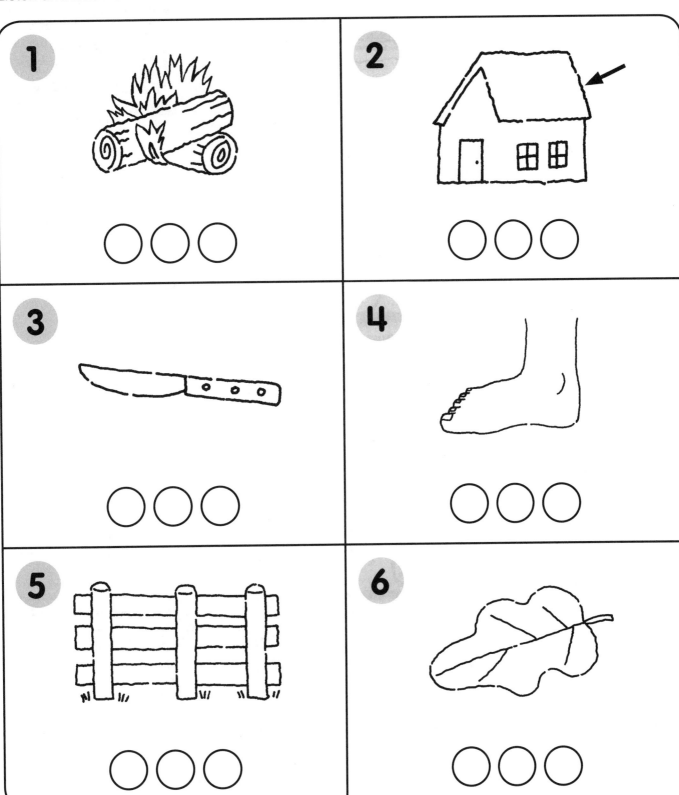

Name _____

What I Learned

Concept
Stop, drop, and roll if your clothes catch fire.

Oral Vocabulary

drop	roll
firefighter	safety
flames	stop

To Parents
This week, your child listened to the story "Fire Safety." In the story, a firefighter and his dog visited a school to teach students about fire safety. The students learned to stop, drop, and roll if their clothes catch fire. Spot the dog showed them his trick—he can stop, drop, and roll, too!

What to Do
Have your child tell you what is happening in the picture. Ask your child to tell you what to do if his or her clothes catch fire. Then have your child demonstrate how to stop, drop, and roll to put out the flames. Have him or her color the picture.

What to Do Next
Help your child determine how to leave the house if there is a fire. In addition, establish a meeting place for everyone in the family to go to in case of a fire emergency. Hold a fire drill to practice getting to that place.

Everyday Literacy: Listening and Speaking • EMC 2415 • © Evan-Moor Corp.

WEEK 11

Concept

An act of kindness will come back to you.

The Lion and the Mouse

Oral Vocabulary

Naming words: kind, lion, mouse

Action words: chew, roar

Describing words: big, tiny

Day 1

SKILLS:

Listening and Speaking

• Respond appropriately to directions and questions

• Speak in complete sentences

• Take turns speaking in a group

• Follow directions

• Use new vocabulary

• Relate new vocabulary to prior knowledge

• Speak audibly

• Listen for different purposes

• Interpret illustrations

Comprehension

• Make inferences and draw conclusions

• Note details

• Recall details

Listening to the Story

Distribute the Day 1 picture to each student. Then read aloud the story below. Ask students to listen carefully as you read.

Long ago, a lion was napping in the forest. Something tickled his nose. "Roar!" He trapped a mouse with his big paw.

The mouse said, "I'm very sorry, sir. If you don't harm me, then someday I will help you in return."

The lion laughed. "How could a tiny mouse help a big lion?" He yawned and let the mouse go.

One day, not long after, the lion fell into a hunter's net. Although he struggled and roared, he could not get free. The mouse went to see what was wrong. He chewed a hole in the net and set the lion free. You see, when you are kind, someone will be kind to you.

Making Inferences

Guide students in looking at the picture and discussing the story. Use the questions below to help students make connections and inferences.

• *Did the lion think he would ever need a mouse's help? Why or why not?*

• *How was the lion kind to the mouse?*

• *How was the mouse kind to the lion?*

Following Directions

Have students look at the picture. Then say:

Listen carefully and follow my directions.

Day 1 picture

• *What is the lion doing?* (talking to the mouse) *What tickled the lion's nose?* (The mouse tickled the lion's nose.) *Make a black dot on the lion's nose. Make a yellow dot on the lion's paws.*

• *Where are the lion and the mouse?* (in the forest) *What does the mouse want the lion to do?* (let him go) *Make a brown dot on the mouse. Make a green dot on a tree in the forest.*

Have students color the picture according to the dots they made.

Day 2

SKILLS:

Listening and Speaking
- Speak in complete sentences
- Use new vocabulary
- Interpret illustrations
- Listen for different purposes
- Take turns speaking in a group

Comprehension
- Identify beginning, middle, and end of a story
- Retell a story
- Recall details

Motor Skills
- Develop small muscle coordination

Retelling a Story

Reread the Day 1 story if necessary. Then distribute the Day 2 activity. Say:

Listen carefully and follow my directions.

- *Box 1 shows the beginning of the story. What is happening in the picture?* (A lion is napping. A mouse tickles the lion's nose.) *Finish the picture by drawing a tail on the mouse.*

- *Box 2 shows what happens next. What is happening in the picture?* (The lion catches the mouse. The mouse asks the lion to let him go. The mouse promises to help the lion.) *Finish the picture by drawing a tail on the lion.*

- *Box 3 shows what happens next. What is happening in the picture?* (The lion lets the mouse go.) *Draw the mouse's front and back legs.*

- *Box 4 shows the end of the story. How does the story end? What is happening in the picture?* (The lion falls into a hunter's net. The mouse chews a hole in the net and sets the lion free.) *Look at the word below the picture. It says e–n–d. Say the word with me: end. Now trace the word.*

Have students take turns "reading" the pictures to tell the story to a partner.

Day 2 activity

Day 3

SKILLS:

Listening and Speaking
- Follow directions
- Listen for different purposes
- Interpret illustrations
- Use new vocabulary

Comprehension
- Recall details

Phonological Awareness
- Blend a word when orally divided into syllables

Blending Syllables

Reread the Day 1 story if necessary. Say:

In our story, a tiny mouse helped a big lion.

- *What surprised you about this story?*

Distribute the Day 3 activity. Then say:

Listen carefully and follow my directions.

- *I will say a word in two parts. Listen: kind•ness. The word is kindness. Now it's your turn.* (**kindness**)

- *Look at box 1. Listen and tell me the word: li•on. What is the word?* (**lion**) *Circle the lion.*

- *Look at box 2. Listen and tell me the word: for•est. What is the word?* (**forest**) *Circle the forest.*

- *Look at box 3. Listen and tell me the word: ti•ny. What is the word?* (**tiny**) *Circle the one that is tiny.*

- *Look at box 4. Listen and tell me the word: hunt•er. What is the word?* (**hunter**) *Circle the hunter.*

Day 3 activity

Everyday Literacy: Listening and Speaking • EMC 2415 • © Evan-Moor Corp.

SKILLS:

Listening and Speaking
- Describe people, places, things, locations, and actions
- Identify a wide variety of objects
- Follow directions
- Take turns speaking in a group
- Interpret illustrations
- Listen for different purposes
- Use new vocabulary

Comprehension
- Compare and contrast
- Note details
- Recall details

Using Word Opposites

Reread the Day 1 story if necessary. Say:

In our story, a tiny mouse helped a big lion.

- *How are the lion and the mouse different?*
- *How are they the same?*

Distribute the Day 4 activity. Then say:

Listen carefully and follow my directions.

- *Name the pictures in box 1.* (**lion**, **mouse**) *Which animal is big and which animal is tiny?* (lion is big, mouse is tiny) *Draw a blue circle around the big animal. Draw a red line under the tiny animal.*

- *Name the pictures in box 2.* (**flower**, **tree**) *Which one is large and which one is small?* (tree is large, flower is small) *Draw a green circle around the large one. Draw an orange line under the small one.*

- *Name the pictures in box 3.* (**baby**, **man**) *Which person is young and which person is old?* (baby is young, man is old) *Draw a brown circle around the young person. Draw a yellow line under the old person.*

- *Name the pictures in box 4.* (**ant**, **elephant**) *Which one is little and which one is huge?* (ant is little, elephant is huge) *Draw a purple circle around the little one. Draw a black line under the huge one.*

Day 4 activity

SKILLS:

Listening and Speaking
- Recite short poems, rhymes, and songs
- Use new vocabulary
- Take turns speaking in a group
- Develop auditory memory

Comprehension
- Recall details

Motor Skills
- Develop large muscle coordination

Home–School Connection p. 98
Spanish version available (see p. 2)

Circle Activity

Have students sit in a circle on the rug. Then review the concepts and vocabulary they practiced this week. Ask:

- *How was the lion kind to the mouse?*
- *How did the mouse save the lion from the hunter's net?*
- *Why did the mouse save the lion?*

Teach this song, sung to the tune of "Row, Row, Row Your Boat." Turn to the student on your right and shake his or her hand. Then have that student turn to the right and do the same thing. Have students continue to turn and shake hands with the child to their right until the song ends. See how quickly the handshake can travel around the circle.

Round, round, round we go.
The circle goes around.
A kind act comes back to you.
The circle goes around.

Extend the Activity

Have students tell about a time they were kind to someone.

Name _____

The Lion and the Mouse

Name _____

The Lion and the Mouse

Finish the pictures. Tell the story.

end

Name _____

The Lion and the Mouse

Listen to the word parts. Circle the answer.

1

2

3

4

Everyday Literacy: Listening and Speaking • EMC 2415 • © Evan-Moor Corp.

Name _____

The Lion and the Mouse

Listen and follow the directions.

Name _____

What I Learned

To Parents

This week, your child listened to the story "The Lion and the Mouse." In this classic fable, a tiny mouse awakens a sleeping lion. The lion catches the mouse but lets him go after the mouse promises to someday help the lion in return. When the lion falls into a hunter's net, the mouse chews a hole in it and frees the lion.

What to Do

Have your child tell you the story below. Point to one picture at a time and have him or her explain what is happening. Encourage your child to use the vocabulary words in the box. Then have him or her color the pictures.

Concept

An act of kindness will come back to you.

Oral Vocabulary

big	mouse
chew	roar
kind	tiny
lion	

What to Do Next

Make a lion puppet and a mouse puppet with your child. Trace a lion and a mouse from the story. Then draw a circle around each one and help your child cut out the circles. Next, glue the pictures on paper rings that fit your child's fingers. Then show him or her how to use the finger puppets to act out the story.

Everyday Literacy: Listening and Speaking • EMC 2415 • © Evan-Moor Corp.

Family Picnic

Oral Vocabulary

Naming words: bone, cookie, family, food, park, picnic
Action word: run

SKILLS:

**Listening and
Speaking**
• Respond
appropriately to
directions and
questions
• Speak in complete
sentences
• Take turns speaking
in a group
• Follow directions
• Use new vocabulary
• Relate new
vocabulary to prior
knowledge
• Speak audibly
• Describe ideas,
feelings, and
experiences
• Interpret illustrations
• Listen for different
purposes

Comprehension
• Make inferences and
draw conclusions
• Note details
• Recall details
• Respond to open-
ended questions
• Make connections
using illustrations
and real-life
experiences

Listening to the Story

Distribute the Day 1 picture to each student. Then read aloud the story below.
Ask students to listen carefully as you read.

*Hi! My name is Leon. On special days, my family likes to go on a
picnic. We all pile into the car and head for the park. The park is great
because there is a lot of space to play. Zip loves to grab a stick and
run across the grass. The best part of visiting the park is sitting down
at a picnic table and eating lunch together. Mom always packs a lot
of food in our picnic basket, and Grandma always bakes the best
cookies. Mom never forgets to bring a bone for Zip. My family loves
to picnic in the park.*

Making Inferences

Guide students in looking at the picture and
discussing the story. Use the questions below to
help students make connections and inferences.

• *Who is Zip?*
• *Who are Leon's family members?*

Following Directions

Have students look at the picture. Then say:
Listen carefully and follow my directions.

Day 1 picture

• *What does Leon's family do on special days?*
(go on a picnic) *Have you ever been on a
picnic? What did you eat?* (Answers vary.)

• *What does Leon's grandma make for the picnics?* (cookies) *Make a
brown dot on the picnic basket. Make a yellow dot on the cookies.*

• *How many children are in Leon's family?* (three) *How many grown-ups
are in his family?* (four) *Make a red dot on each child. Make a blue dot
on each grown-up.*

• *What does Zip like to do at the park?* (grab a stick and run) *Make
a black dot on Zip.*

Have students color the picture according to the dots they made.

Day 2

SKILLS:

Listening and Speaking
- Speak audibly
- Speak in complete sentences
- Describe people, places, things, locations, and actions
- Use new vocabulary
- Follow directions
- Interpret illustrations
- Listen for different purposes
- Respond appropriately to directions and questions

Comprehension
- Note details
- Recall details

Recalling the Story

Guide a discussion that helps students recall the Day 1 story. Reread the story if necessary. Say:

Our story is about a family that likes to have picnics in the park.

- *Why does the family go on picnics?*
- *Why is the park a good place for picnics?*

Distribute the Day 2 activity. Then say:

Listen carefully and follow my directions.

- *What do you see in box 1?* (Grandma with cookies) *Does Grandma make cookies for family picnics? Color the happy face for **yes** or the sad face for **no**.* (yes)

- *What do you see in box 2?* (children swimming) *Does that happen in the story? Color the happy face for **yes** or the sad face for **no**.* (no)

- *What do you see in box 3?* (Zip running with a stick) *Does that happen in the story? Color the happy face for **yes** or the sad face for **no**.* (yes)

- *What do you see in box 4?* (family eating together) *Does that happen in the story? Color the happy face for **yes** or the sad face for **no**.* (yes) *Where would you like to have a picnic? What would you like to eat?* (Answers vary.)

Day 2 activity

Day 3

SKILLS:

Listening and Speaking
- Follow directions
- Listen for different purposes
- Identify a wide variety of objects

Comprehension
- Recall details

Phonological Awareness
- Break a spoken word into separate phonemes
- Identify and count phonemes

Listening for Phonemes

Reread the Day 1 story if necessary. Say:

Our story is about a family's picnics in the park.

- *What does Zip love to do at the park?*

Distribute the Day 3 activity. Then say:

I will say a word. Then I will stretch it, sound by sound. I will tell you how many sounds I hear.

- *Listen: **food**. /f-oo-d/. I hear three sounds in the word **food**. Now it's your turn.*

- *Look at box 1. Name the picture.* (**Leon**) *Now let's stretch it, sound by sound: /l-ē-ŏ-n/. How many sounds do you hear?* (four) *Circle the number **4**.*

- *Look at box 2. Name the picture.* (**Zip**) *Now stretch it, sound by sound: /z-ī-p/. How many sounds do you hear?* (three) *Circle the number **3**.*

- *Look at box 3. Name the picture.* (**cookie**) *Now stretch it, sound by sound: /k-oo-k-e/. How many sounds do you hear?* (four) *Circle the number **4**.*

- *Look at box 4. Name the picture.* (**bone**) *Now stretch it, sound by sound: /b-ō-n/. How many sounds do you hear?* (three) *Circle the number **3**.*

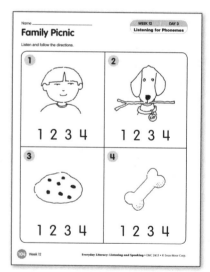

Day 3 activity

Day 4

SKILLS:

Listening and Speaking
- Identify and sort common words into basic categories
- Identify a wide variety of objects
- Follow directions
- Interpret illustrations
- Listen for different purposes
- Develop auditory memory
- Respond appropriately to directions and questions

Comprehension
- Make inferences and draw conclusions
- Categorize and classify
- Recall details
- Make connections using illustrations and real-life experiences

Using Auditory Memory

Reread the Day 1 story if necessary. Say:

In our story, a boy tells about what his family likes to do on special days.

- *Where does Leon's family eat when they're at the park?*
- *What does Leon's mom always bring for Zip?*

Distribute the Day 4 activity. Then say:

Listen carefully and follow my directions.

- *Look at row 1. Which things would you bring to a picnic?* (sandwich, lemonade, fruit) *Draw lines under the sandwich, lemonade, and fruit. Which one wouldn't you bring? Why?*

- *Look at row 2. Which things can a family use at a picnic in the park?* (table, barbecue, lawn chair) *Draw lines under the table, barbecue, and lawn chair. Which one can't they use? Why?*

- *Look at row 3. Which things can the children do at a park?* (eat cookies, swing, play baseball) *Draw lines under Leon eating a cookie, the swings, and the baseball mitt. Which one can't the children do at a park? Why?*

- *Look at row 4. Which of these things would Leon bring to the park for his dog Zip?* (leash, dog bowl, bone) *Draw lines under the leash, dog bowl, and bone. Which one wouldn't Leon bring to the park for Zip? Why?*

Day 4 activity

Day 5

SKILLS:

Listening and Speaking
- Recite short poems, rhymes, and songs
- Use new vocabulary
- Describe ideas, feelings, and experiences
- Develop auditory memory

Home–School Connection p. 106
Spanish version available (see p. 2)

Circle Activity

Have students sit in a circle on the rug. Then connect the story to students' lives by asking:

- *Have you ever been on a picnic? What did you eat? What did you play?*
- *What do you and your family do together on special days?*

Introduce the chant below by reading the first two lines and having the class echo you. Then model completing the sentence frame. Go around the circle, with the class chanting the first two lines together and each student taking a turn completing the sentence frame.

Chant together: *I love my family.*
My family loves me.

Student: *When we're together, we _____.*

Extend the Activity

Have students share their favorite memories of being with their families.

Name _____

Family Picnic

Name _____

Family Picnic

Did it happen in the story?

1

 yes   ☹ no

2

 yes   ☹ no

3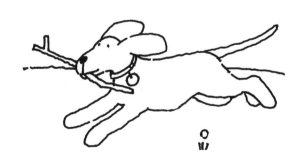

 yes   ☹ no

4

 yes   ☹ no

Name _____

Family Picnic

Listen and follow the directions.

1

1 2 3 4

2

1 2 3 4

3

1 2 3 4

4

1 2 3 4

Everyday Literacy: Listening and Speaking • EMC 2415 • © Evan-Moor Corp.

Family Picnic

Listen and follow the directions.

   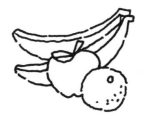 

Name _____

What I Learned

To Parents

This week, your child listened to the story "Family Picnic." In the story, Leon tells about how his family enjoys picnics in the park. The kids love to play. The dog grabs a stick and runs across the grass. Leon's favorite part of the day is sitting with his family and eating the yummy food packed in the basket.

What to Do

Have your child tell you about this week's story. Ask: **What is Leon's favorite part of the picnic?** Then have your child tell you his or her favorite family activity and draw a picture of it. Ask your child to tell you about the picture that he or she drew.

Concept
Families have fun together.

Oral Vocabulary

bone   park
cookie   picnic
family   run
food

I have fun with my family.

What to Do Next

Prepare a simple picnic with your child. Enjoy it together outdoors if weather permits. If not, have fun picnicking indoors!

Everyday Literacy: Listening and Speaking • EMC 2415 • © Evan-Moor Corp.

Jack and Jill

Oral Vocabulary

Naming words: crown, hill, nursery rhyme

Describing words: down, up

Day 1

SKILLS:

Listening and Speaking
- Use new vocabulary
- Speak audibly
- Take turns speaking in groups
- Relate new vocabulary to prior knowledge
- Follow directions
- Recite short poems, rhymes, and songs
- Interpret illustrations
- Respond appropriately to directions and questions
- Speak in complete sentences
- Identify a wide variety of objects
- Listen for different purposes

Comprehension
- Make inferences and draw conclusions
- Distinguish between real and make-believe
- Respond to open-ended questions
- Note details
- Recall details

Listening to the Rhyme

Distribute the Day 1 picture to each student. Then say: *We are going to listen to a nursery rhyme. Nursery rhymes are fun to listen to because they have rhyming words. Rhyming words are words that have the same ending sound.* **Top** *and* **pop** *are rhyming words.* Then read aloud the rhyme below. Ask students to listen carefully as you read.

Mother Goose has come to say hello
With nursery rhyme friends you just might know.
So listen to her and take a closer look
At two young friends from her famous book.

Jack and Jill went up the hill
To fetch a pail of water.
Jack fell down and broke his crown,
And Jill came tumbling after.

Making Inferences

Guide students in looking at the picture and discussing the rhyme. Use the questions below to help students make connections and inferences.

- *Is Mother Goose real or make-believe?*
- *Why are nursery rhymes fun to listen to?*

Following Directions

Have students look at the picture. Then say:

Listen carefully and follow my directions.

- *Point to Mother Goose. Now point to Jack and Jill. Repeat the nursery rhyme after me. (Read the rhyme one line at a time.) Draw a blue circle around Mother Goose. Draw a red line under Jack and Jill.*
- *Why did Jack and Jill go up the hill?* (to fetch a pail of water) *What was on top of the hill?* (a well, water) *Make a yellow dot on the well.*
- *Why do you think Jack fell down?* (Answers vary.) *Draw Jack falling down the hill.*

Have students color the picture.

Day 1 picture

Day 2

SKILLS:

Listening and Speaking
- Recite short poems, rhymes, and songs
- Speak in complete sentences
- Follow directions
- Listen for different purposes
- Interpret illustrations

Comprehension
- Identify a sequence of events
- Recall details

Motor Skills
- Develop small muscle coordination

Sequencing

Guide a discussion that helps students recall the Day 1 rhyme. Reread the rhyme if necessary. Say:

We listened to a nursery rhyme.

- *Why did Jack and Jill go up the hill?*

Distribute the Day 2 activity. Then say:

Listen carefully and follow my directions.

- *The pictures show the nursery rhyme "Jack and Jill." Let's say the rhyme together: "Jack and Jill went up the hill / to fetch a pail of water. / Jack fell down and broke his crown, / and Jill came tumbling after."*

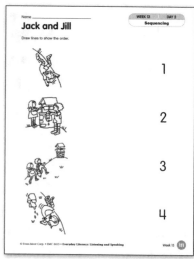

Day 2 activity

- *Look at the pictures. Which one shows what happened first in the rhyme?* (Jack and Jill going up the hill) *Put your pencil on the picture of Jack and Jill going up the hill. Draw a line to the number **1**.*

- *What did Jack and Jill do at the top of the hill?* (got a pail of water) *Put your pencil on the picture of them getting water. Draw a line to the number **2**.*

- *Then what happened to Jack?* (fell down and broke his crown) *Put your pencil on the picture of Jack falling down. Draw a line to the number **3**.*

- *What happened last?* (Jill came tumbling after.) *Put your pencil on the picture of Jill tumbling down. Draw a line to the number **4**.*

Day 3

SKILLS:

Speaking and Listening
- Respond appropriately to directions and questions
- Use new vocabulary
- Follow directions
- Listen for different purposes
- Identify a wide variety of objects

Phonological Awareness
- Recognize words that rhyme

Listening for Rhyme

Recite "Jack and Jill" together. Then say:

*Remember, nursery rhymes are fun to listen to because they have rhyming words. Rhyming words are words that have the same ending sound. **Top** and **pop** are rhyming words.*

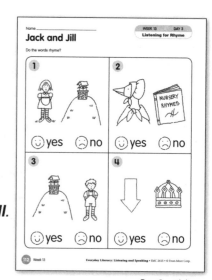

Day 3 activity

Distribute the Day 3 activity. Then say:

Listen carefully and follow my directions.

- *Name the pictures in box 1 with me: **Jill, hill**. Do they rhyme? Color the happy face for **yes** or the sad face for **no**.* (yes) *Can you name another word that rhymes with **Jill**?* (**bill, mill, will**, etc.)

- *Name the pictures in box 2 with me: **goose, book**. Do they rhyme? Color the happy face for **yes** or the sad face for **no**.* (no)

- *Name the pictures in box 3 with me: **hill, Jack**. Do they rhyme? Color the happy face for **yes** or the sad face for **no**.* (no)

- *Name the pictures in box 4 with me: **down, crown**. Do they rhyme? Color the happy face for **yes** or the sad face for **no**.* (yes)

Using Positional Words

Recite "Jack and Jill" together. Then distribute the Day 4 activity. Say:

Listen carefully and follow my directions.

- *Put your finger on the first word above the drawing. It says **up**. Say it with me: **up**. Trace the word **up**. Then look for the arrow that points up the hill. Trace the arrow that points up the hill.*

- *Now put your finger on the next word above the drawing. It says **down**. Say it with me: **down**. Trace the word **down**. Then look for the arrow that points down the hill. Trace the arrow that points down the hill.*

*Now let's recite the nursery rhyme together again. When we say the word **up**, we will use our finger to point up. When we say the word **down**, we will use our finger to point down.*

Repeat the rhyme, having students respond to the words **up** and **down** in various ways such as looking up and looking down, standing up and kneeling down, etc. Then have students color the picture.

Day 4 activity

Circle Activity

Have students sit in a circle on the rug. Then review the concepts and vocabulary they practiced this week. Recite "Jack and Jill" together, emphasizing the rhyming words. Ask:

- *Which words rhyme in "Jack and Jill"?*

Turn "Jack and Jill" into a follow-the-leader activity. Have students stand in a line. Act as the leader, guiding students in simple actions that help them to "act out" the rhyme.

Jack and Jill went up the hill (March in line.)

To fetch a pail of water. (Hold arms open as if carrying a pail.)

Jack fell down and broke his crown, (Fall down to the ground; hold head.)

And Jill came tumbling after. (Roll hands in front of body.)

Have students take turns being the leader. Encourage them to think of new actions for each line of the rhyme.

Extend the Activity

Read aloud from a book of nursery rhymes. Take requests! Ask students to name their favorites for you to read. Then select some lesser-known rhymes to read to them. Occasionally, ask students to name the words that rhyme.

Jack and Jill

Everyday Literacy: Listening and Speaking • EMC 2415 • © Evan-Moor Corp.

Name _____

Jack and Jill

Draw lines to show the order.

1

2

3

4

Jack and Jill

Do the words rhyme?

1. ☺ yes   ☹ no
2. ☺ yes   ☹ no
3. ☺ yes   ☹ no
4. ☺ yes   ☹ no

Name _____

Jack and Jill

Listen and follow the directions.

up   down

Name _____

What I Learned

To Parents

This week, your child listened to the nursery rhyme "Jack and Jill."

Jack and Jill went up the hill
To fetch a pail of water.
Jack fell down and broke his crown,
And Jill came tumbling after.

What to Do

Recite the rhyme with your child. Then have him or her tell you what is happening in the picture. Encourage your child to use the vocabulary words in the box.

Concept
Nursery rhymes are fun to say.

Oral Vocabulary

crown	nursery rhyme
down	up
hill	

What to Do Next

Read a book of nursery rhymes together. Have your child name some of the rhyming word pairs he or she hears. Challenge your child to learn a nursery rhyme by heart.

Everyday Literacy: Listening and Speaking • EMC 2415 • © Evan-Moor Corp.

Concept

Five senses tell us about the world.

My Five Senses

Oral Vocabulary

Naming words: bird, flowers, kitten, senses, strawberry, sun

Action words: hear, see, smell, taste, touch

Day 1

SKILLS:

Listening and Speaking

• Use new vocabulary
• Follow directions
• Speak audibly
• Take turns speaking in a group
• Respond appropriately to directions and questions
• Interpret illustrations
• Use language to show reasoning
• Identify a wide variety of objects
• Speak in complete sentences
• Relate new vocabulary to prior knowledge
• Develop auditory memory

Comprehension

• Make inferences and draw conclusions
• Recall details
• Note details
• Make connections using illustrations, prior knowledge, and real-life experiences

Listening to the Story

Distribute the Day 1 picture to each student. Say: *We have five senses. We see, hear, smell, touch, and taste things in the world around us.* Then read aloud the story below. Point to each body part as you name it. Ask students to listen carefully as you read.

Hi, my name is Ben. Did you know that we use our five senses every day? My five senses tell me all about my world:

My eyes let me see the sun in the sky.
My ears let me hear the call of the bluebird.
My nose lets me smell the flowers that grow.
My hands let me touch the soft, warm fur of my kitten.
My mouth lets me taste the sweet strawberry.
My five senses are amazing!

Making Inferences

Guide students in looking at the picture and discussing the story. Use the questions below to help students make connections and inferences.

• *Which sense tells Ben how a bird sounds?*
• *Which sense tells Ben how food tastes?*

Following Directions

Have students look at the picture. Then say:

Listen carefully and follow my directions.

• *What does Ben use to see the sun?* (eyes) *Make a yellow dot on the sun and on Ben's eyes.*

• *What does Ben use to hear the bird?* (ears) *Make a blue dot on the bird and on Ben's ears.*

• *What does Ben use to smell the flowers?* (nose) *Make a purple dot on the flowers and on Ben's nose.*

• *What does Ben use to touch his kitten?* (hand) *Make a brown dot on the kitten and on Ben's hand.*

• *What does Ben use to taste the strawberry?* (mouth) *Make a red dot on the strawberry and on Ben's mouth.*

Day 1 picture

SKILLS:

Listening and Speaking
- Identify and sort common words into basic categories
- Use new vocabulary
- Respond appropriately to directions and questions
- Follow directions
- Identify a wide variety of objects

Comprehension
- Categorize and classify
- Make connections using illustrations and real-life experiences

Identifying Senses

Guide a discussion that helps students recall the Day 1 story. Reread the story if necessary. Say:

We use our five senses to see, hear, smell, touch, and taste. Our senses help us know about the world.

Distribute the Day 2 activity. Then say:

Listen carefully and follow my directions.

Day 2 activity

- *Point to the ear. What can you do with your ears?* (hear) *Name the pictures in this row.* (**bird**, **bell**, **watermelon**) *Draw a blue line under the things you can hear.* (bird, bell)

- *Point to the nose. What can you do with your nose?* (smell) *Name the pictures in this row.* (**flower**, **cloud**, **skunk**) *Draw an orange line under the things you can smell.* (flower, skunk)

- *Point to the hand. What can you do with your hands?* (touch) *Name the pictures in this row.* (**kitten**, **stones**, **cloud**) *Draw a green line under the things you can touch.* (kitten, stones)

- *Point to the mouth. What can you do with your mouth?* (taste) *Name the pictures in this row.* (**sandwich**, **sun**, **strawberry**) *Draw a red line under the things you can taste.* (sandwich, strawberry)

- *Point to the eye. What can you do with your eyes?* (see) *Name the pictures in this row.* (**sun**, **butterfly**, **music notes**) *Draw a black line under the things you can see.* (sun, butterfly)

Day 3

SKILLS:

Listening and Speaking
- Follow directions
- Listen for different purposes

Phonological Awareness
- Identify common beginning consonant sounds in spoken words
- Identify common ending consonant sounds in spoken words
- Identify common medial consonant sounds in spoken words

Listening for Consonant Sounds

Reread the Day 1 story. Then distribute the Day 3 activity. Ask:

What body part are you using when you listen? (ears) *Yes, now use your ears to follow directions.*

Day 3 activity

- *Look at box 1. Name the picture.* (**Ben**) *Stretch his name with me: /B-ĕ-n/. Do you hear /n/ at the beginning, middle, or end of **Ben**?* (end) *Fill in the last circle.*

- *Look at box 2. Name the picture.* (**nose**) *Stretch the word: /n-ō-z/. Do you hear /n/ at the beginning, middle, or end of **nose**?* (beginning) *Fill in the first circle.*

- *Look at box 3. Name the picture.* (**kitten**) *Stretch the word: /k-ĭ-t-ĕ-n/. Do you hear /n/ at the beginning, middle, or end of **kitten**?* (end) *Fill in the last circle.*

- *Look at box 4. Name the picture.* (**hand**) *Stretch the word: /h-ă-n-d/. Do you hear /n/ at the beginning, middle, or end of **hand**?* (middle) *Fill in the middle circle.*

Day 4

SKILLS:

Listening and Speaking
• Listen for different purposes
• Speak in complete sentences
• Follow directions
• Identify a wide variety of objects

Comprehension
• Retell a story
• Recall details
• Make inferences and draw conclusions

Motor Skills
• Develop small muscle coordination

Following Directions

Reread the Day 1 story. Then distribute the Day 4 activity. Say:

One day, Ben's big brother took him to the fair. Let's draw a path to show what they did there. Listen carefully and follow my directions.

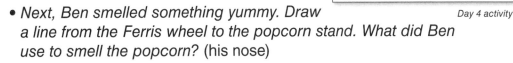

Day 4 activity

• *Start by putting your pencil on Ben.*

• *First, Ben and his brother rode the Ferris wheel. Draw a line from Ben to the Ferris wheel. Ben could see the entire fair from the Ferris wheel! What did Ben use to see the fair?* (his eyes)

• *Next, Ben smelled something yummy. Draw a line from the Ferris wheel to the popcorn stand. What did Ben use to smell the popcorn?* (his nose)

• *Then, Ben heard music. Draw a line from the popcorn stand to the stage. What did Ben use to hear the music?* (his ears)

• *Ben was getting thirsty, so his brother bought him some lemonade. Draw a line from the stage to the lemonade stand. What did Ben use to taste the lemonade?* (his mouth)

• *Finally, Ben got to pet a lamb. Draw a line from the lemonade stand to the barn. What did Ben use to touch the soft lamb?* (his hands)

Have students use the path they drew to retell the story to a partner.

Day 5

SKILLS:

Listening and Speaking
• Take turns speaking in a group
• Speak in complete sentences
• Recite short poems, rhymes, and songs
• Use new vocabulary

Home–School Connection p.122
Spanish version available (see p. 2)

Circle Activity

Have students sit in a circle on the rug. Review the concepts and vocabulary they practiced this week. Say:

• *Let's point to each body part as we name our five senses: see, hear, smell, touch, taste.*

Introduce and model the song below, sung to the tune of "London Bridge." Then model how to complete the sentence frame in each verse. As students sing the song, allow each student to complete a sentence frame.

What do you see with your eyes? with your eyes? with your eyes?
What do you see with your eyes? Tell us, (student's name).
Student: *I see _____.*

What do you hear with your ears? with your ears? with your ears?
What do you hear with your ears? Tell us, (student's name).
Student: *I hear _____.*

What do you smell with your nose?… Student: I smell _____.

What do you taste with your mouth?… Student: I taste _____.

What do you touch with your hands?… Student: I touch _____.

Name _____

My Five Senses

Name _____

My Five Senses

Listen and follow the directions.

 |

 |

 |

 |

 |

My Five Senses

Listen and follow the directions.

1

◯ ◯ ◯

2

◯ ◯ ◯

3

◯ ◯ ◯

4

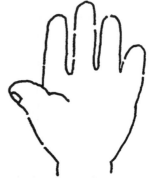

◯ ◯ ◯

Everyday Literacy: Listening and Speaking • EMC 2415 • © Evan-Moor Corp.

Name _____

My Five Senses

Listen and draw a path.

Name _____

What I Learned

To Parents
This week, your child listened to the story "My Five Senses." In the story, Ben sees the sun, hears a bluebird, smells the flowers, touches the fur of a kitten, and tastes a strawberry. He thinks his senses are amazing!

What to Do
Have your child name the five senses and the body part each sense is connected to (e.g., smell/nose). Then have your child look at each object in the picture and name all of the senses he or she can use to know about that object. Ask questions such as: **Which senses can you use to know about the sun?**

Concept
Five senses tell us about the world.

Oral Vocabulary
bird	smell
flowers	strawberry
hear	sun
kitten	taste
see	touch
senses	

What to Do Next
Bake cookies with your child. Baking is an activity that can involve all the senses. While you bake, ask your child to name the things he or she senses (for example, "I see yellow egg yolks, feel sticky dough, hear a loud mixer, smell cookies baking, and taste delicious cookies.").

Everyday Literacy: Listening and Speaking • EMC 2415 • © Evan-Moor Corp.

Healthy Teeth

Oral Vocabulary

Naming words: cavities, dentist, teeth, toothbrush

Action word: brush

Describing word: healthy

SKILLS:

Listening and Speaking
- Use new vocabulary
- Follow directions
- Respond appropriately to directions and questions
- Speak audibly
- Take turns speaking in a group
- Interpret illustrations
- Relate new vocabulary to prior knowledge
- Speak in complete sentences

Comprehension
- Make inferences and draw conclusions
- Note details
- Recall details
- Respond to open-ended questions
- Make connections using illustrations and real-life experiences

Listening to the Story

Distribute the Day 1 picture to each student. Then read aloud the story below. Ask students to listen carefully as you read.

> *Yesterday, I visited Dr. Marks. He is a dentist. Dr. Marks checked my teeth to make sure they are healthy. He counted my teeth and looked for cavities. Dr. Marks said I have healthy teeth. I do a good job of brushing, and I didn't have any cavities. Dr. Marks gave me a new toothbrush. I said "Thank you" and gave him a big smile.*

Making Inferences

Guide students in looking at the picture and discussing the story. Use the questions below to help students make connections and inferences.

- *Who is Dr. Marks?*
- *What does a dentist do?*
- *How can you keep your teeth healthy?*

Following Directions

Have students look at the picture. Then say:

Listen carefully and follow my directions.

Day 1 picture

- *What is the girl doing in the picture?* (She is visiting the dentist.) *How do you know that she is at a dentist's office?* (She is sitting in a dentist's chair.) *Do you visit a dentist?* (Answers vary.) *Make a green dot on the girl. Make a blue dot on the dentist's chair.*

- *What is the dentist giving the girl?* (a new toothbrush) *What is a toothbrush used for?* (brushing your teeth) *Why should you brush your teeth?* (to keep them healthy) *Make a purple dot on Dr. Marks. Draw a red circle around the toothbrush. What color is your toothbrush?* (Answers vary.)

- *Point to the giant tooth. Do you know how many times a day you should brush your teeth?* (at least two times) *Draw a red circle around the giant tooth.*

Have students color the picture according to the dots they made.

SKILLS:

Listening and Speaking
• Identify a wide variety of objects
• Speak in complete sentences
• Respond appropriately to directions and questions
• Follow directions

Comprehension
• Note details
• Recall details

Recalling the Story

Guide a discussion that helps students recall the Day 1 story. Reread the story if necessary. Say:

We listened to a story about a girl who visited the dentist.

> • *How did the girl help to keep away cavities?*

Distribute the Day 2 activity. Then say:

Listen carefully and follow my directions.

> • *Look at row 1. Name the pictures. (***desk***, ***dentist's chair***, ***highchair***) In our story, where did the girl sit? (dentist's chair) Draw a red line under the dentist's chair.*

> • *Look at row 2. Name the pictures. (***dentist***, ***hairstylist***, ***firefighter***) In our story, whom did the girl visit? (dentist) Draw a purple line under the dentist.*

> • *Look at row 3. Name the pictures. (***eyes***, ***teeth***, ***feet***) In our story, what did Dr. Marks check? (teeth) Draw a green line under the teeth.*

> • *Look at row 4. Name the pictures. (***doll***, ***lunch***, ***toothbrush***) What did Dr. Marks give the girl? (toothbrush) Draw a blue line under the toothbrush.*

Day 2 activity

SKILLS:

Listening and Speaking
• Listen for different purposes
• Identify a wide variety of objects
• Follow directions

Comprehension
• Recall details

Phonological Awareness
• Identify medial long vowel sounds in spoken words

Listening for Long Vowel Sounds

Reread the Day 1 story if necessary. Say:

In our story, a girl visited the dentist.

> • *What did the dentist check?*

> • *Are the girl's teeth healthy? Why?*

Distribute the Day 3 activity. Then say:

Listen carefully and follow my directions.

> • *I will say a word. Listen for the /ē/ sound: ***seat***, /s•ē•t/. I hear the /ē/ sound in the middle of ***seat***.*

> • *Let's name the pictures in box 1: ***teeth***, ***toast***. Which word has the /ē/ sound in the middle? (***teeth***) Draw a blue circle around the teeth.*

> • *Let's name the pictures in box 2: ***chair***, ***cheese***. Which word has the /ē/ sound in the middle? (***cheese***) Draw a yellow circle around the cheese.*

> • *Let's name the pictures in box 3: ***brush***, ***beads***. Which word has the /ē/ sound in the middle? (***beads***) Draw a green circle around the beads.*

> • *Let's name the pictures in box 4: ***sleep***, ***smile***. Which word has the /ē/ sound in the middle? (***sleep***) Draw a red circle around the sleeping boy.*

Day 3 activity

SKILLS:

Listening and Speaking
• Use new vocabulary
• Follow directions
• Listen for different purposes

Comprehension
• Recall details

Motor Skills
• Develop small muscle coordination

Finishing a Picture

Reread the Day 1 story if necessary. Say:

The girl in our story visited the dentist.

   • *What does a dentist do?*
   • *What did the dentist give the girl?*

Distribute the Day 4 activity. Then say:

Some things are missing from this picture. Listen carefully and follow my directions.

   • *Find the toothbrush. Trace the lines to finish it. What color is your toothbrush? Color the picture of the toothbrush the same color as yours.*

   • *Find the toothpaste tube. Trace the lines. Toothpaste helps get food off your teeth. How many times should you brush each day?*

   • *Finish the picture so it looks like you. Draw your face and hair. Be sure to show your smile.*

   • *Put your finger on the word below the picture. The word is **smile**. Trace the letters to write the word **smile**. Now say the word with me: **smile**.*

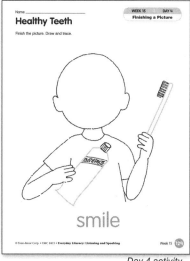

Day 4 activity

SKILLS:

Listening and Speaking
• Recite short poems, rhymes, and songs
• Develop auditory memory
• Take turns speaking in a group

Comprehension
• Recall details

Circle Activity

Have students sit in a circle on the rug. Then review the concepts and vocabulary they practiced this week. Ask:

   • *What did the girl in our story do every day to help keep her teeth healthy?*
   • *Why should you brush your teeth?*
   • *Whom did the girl visit in the story?*
   • *What did the dentist check for?*

Teach students the song below, sung to the tune of "Row, Row, Row Your Boat." Have students make a "brushing" motion as they sing.

Brush, brush, brush your teeth,
Two times every day.
Brush the top, front and back.
Keep cavities away.

Brush, brush, brush your teeth,
Two times every day.
See your dentist for a check.
Healthy teeth—Hooray!

Extend the Activity

Make a class list of things to do to keep teeth healthy: brush twice a day; visit a dentist; eat fruit, vegetables, and cheese for snacks; don't drink sugary soda or eat too many sweets; etc.

Home–School Connection p. 130 Spanish version available (see p. 2)

Name _____

Healthy Teeth

Name _____

Healthy Teeth

Listen and follow the directions.

1

2

3
  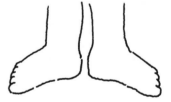

4

Name _____

Healthy Teeth

Listen for the middle sound you hear in **sweet**.

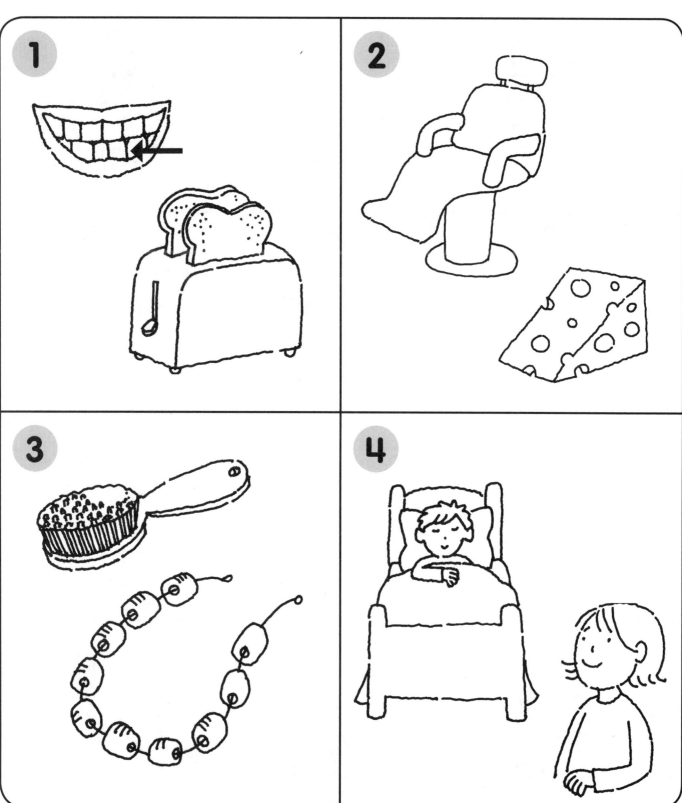

Everyday Literacy: Listening and Speaking • EMC 2415 • © Evan-Moor Corp.

Name _____

Healthy Teeth

Finish the picture. Draw and trace.

smile

Name _____

What I Learned

To Parents

This week, your child listened to the story "Healthy Teeth." In the story, a girl visited the dentist, who counted her teeth and looked for cavities. The girl brushes twice a day, so her teeth are healthy. Before she left his office, the dentist gave her a new toothbrush. She said "Thank you" and gave him a big smile.

Concept
Brush your teeth and visit the dentist.

Oral Vocabulary

brush	healthy
cavities	teeth
dentist	toothbrush

What to Do

Have your child tell you what is happening in the picture. Ask questions such as: **Who is in the picture? What two things does the girl do to keep her teeth healthy? What does a dentist check for?** Encourage your child to use the vocabulary words in the box. Then have him or her color the picture.

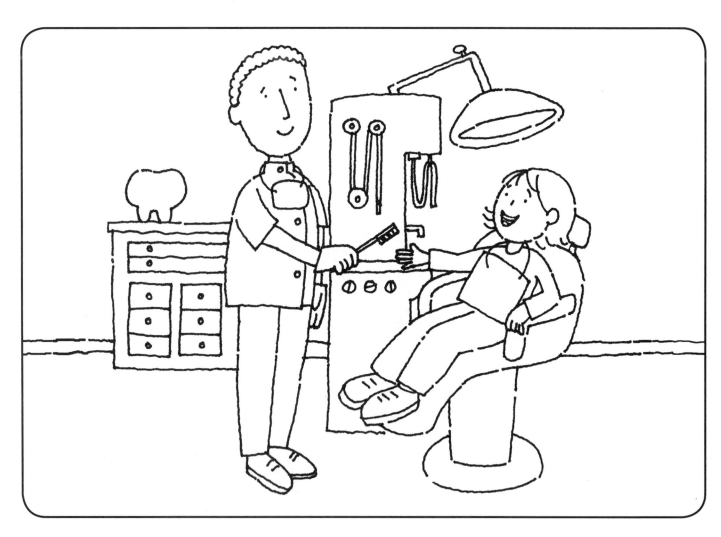

What to Do Next

Make a tooth-brushing chart with your child to encourage brushing twice a day. Write the days of the week and make two spaces to be checked off each day. At the end of each week, give your child an appropriate reward for completing the chart.

Everyday Literacy: Listening and Speaking • EMC 2415 • © Evan-Moor Corp.

Family Night

Oral Vocabulary

Naming words: banjo, family, music, song
Action words: clap, play, sing

Day 1

SKILLS:

**Listening and
Speaking**
• Use new vocabulary
• Relate new
  vocabulary to prior
  knowledge
• Speak in complete
  sentences
• Speak audibly
• Take turns speaking
  in a group
• Follow directions
• Respond
  appropriately to
  directions and
  questions
• Interpret illustrations
• Describe ideas,
  feelings, and
  experiences

Comprehension
• Make inferences and
  draw conclusions
• Note details
• Recall details

Listening to the Story

Distribute the Day 1 picture to each student. Then read aloud the story below. Ask students to listen carefully as you read.

Every Tuesday is family night at my house. My family stays home together and has fun. We play music on our instruments. Dad plays his banjo. Mom plays her guitar. Megan beats her drum. Jon plays his violin. I love the music we make—I clap my hands and sing along! My favorite song is "Oh! Susanna." It is an old song my parents learned when they were young. Family night is fun.

Making Inferences

Guide students in looking at the picture and discussing the story. Use the questions below to help students make connections and inferences.

• *Why do you think Tuesday night is called "family night"?*

• *What other fun things can a family do on family night?*

Following Directions

Have students look at the picture. Then say:
Listen carefully and follow my directions.

Day 1 picture

• *Who plays the banjo in the family?* (Dad) *Make a red dot on Dad. Make an orange dot on the banjo.*

• *What instrument does Mom play?* (guitar) *Make a green dot on Mom. Make a yellow dot on the guitar.*

• *What instrument does Megan play?* (drum) *Make a blue dot on Megan. Make a purple dot on the drum.*

• *Who plays the violin?* (Jon, the brother) *Make a green dot on Jon. Make a brown dot on the violin.*

• *What does the little brother like to do?* (sing and clap) *Make a red dot on the little brother.*

Have students color the picture according to the dots they made.

Day 2

SKILLS:

Listening and Speaking
- Speak in complete sentences
- Respond appropriately to directions and questions
- Use new vocabulary
- Interpret illustrations
- Follow directions
- Describe ideas, feelings, and experiences

Comprehension
- Recall details
- Respond to open-ended questions

Recalling the Story

Guide a discussion that helps students recall the Day 1 story. Reread the story if necessary. Say:

We listened to a story about a family that has fun.

- *How do you have fun with your family?*

Distribute the Day 2 activity. Then say:

Listen carefully and follow my directions.

- *What do you see in box 1?* (a man playing a banjo) *Does that happen in the story? Color the happy face for* **yes** *or the sad face for* **no**. (yes, Dad plays) *What song does Dad play?* ("Oh! Susanna!")

- *What do you see in box 2?* (a girl walking a dog) *Does that happen in the story? Color the happy face for* **yes** *or the sad face for* **no**. (no)

- *What do you see in box 3?* (a boy building with blocks) *Does that happen in the story? Color the happy face for* **yes** *or the sad face for* **no**. (no)

- *What do you see in box 4?* (a lady playing a piano) *Does Mom in the story play a piano? Color the happy face for* **yes** *or the sad face for* **no**. (no) *What instrument does Mom play?* (guitar)

Day 2 activity

Day 3

SKILLS:

Listening and Speaking
- Develop auditory memory
- Follow directions
- Listen for different purposes

Phonological Awareness
- Repeat auditory sequences

Motor Skills
- Develop large muscle coordination

Identifying Rhythms

Reread the Day 1 story if necessary. Then distribute the Day 3 activity. Say:

In the story, the boy likes to clap to the music. Let's see if we can clap in rhythm together. Listen carefully and follow my directions.

- *Look at the pattern next to the number 1. Listen while I clap the pattern.* (Teacher claps pattern.) *I followed the pattern to clap a rhythm. When I see hands clapping, I clap. When I see an empty box, I do not clap.*

- *Let's clap the rhythm next to the number 2 together.* (clap, pause, clap, clap, pause, clap)

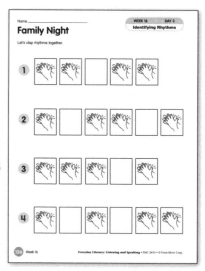

Day 3 activity

Repeat the process for the rhythm patterns next to numbers **3** and **4**.

Extend the Activity

Choose one of the rhythm patterns. Ask students to listen to the rhythm you clap and guess which rhythm pattern it is. Have students circle the number beside the rhythm pattern you clapped.

Everyday Literacy: Listening and Speaking • EMC 2415 • © Evan-Moor Corp.

Day 4

SKILLS:

Listening and Speaking
- Take turns speaking in a group
- Use new vocabulary
- Describe people, places, things, locations and actions
- Interpret illustrations
- Use language to show reasoning
- Describe ideas, feelings, and experiences
- Follow directions

Comprehension
- Make predictions
- Identify sequence of events
- Recall details

Predicting Outcomes

Reread the Day 1 story if necessary. Say:

In our story, a boy and his family spend time together.

> • *Who plays the banjo?*

Distribute the Day 4 activity. Then say:

Listen carefully and follow my directions.

> • *Look at row 1. What is happening in the pictures?* (cooking dinner; sitting at the table) *What do you think will happen next? Why?* (eat dinner because the food is ready; they are at the table) *Draw a line from row 1 to the picture that shows the family eating.*

> • *Look at row 2. What is happening in the pictures?* (Dad is carrying a banjo case; he opens the case.) *What do you think will happen next?* (Dad will play the banjo.) *Draw a line from row 2 to the picture that shows Dad playing the banjo.*

> • *Look at row 3. What is happening in the pictures?* (Boy is building a tower of blocks; tower is really tall, boy is adding one more block.) *What do you think will happen next? Why?* (The tower will fall because it is too tall.) *Draw a line from row 3 to the picture that shows the tower falling.*

Day 4 activity

Day 5

SKILLS:

Listening and Speaking
- Recite short poems, rhymes, and songs
- Use new vocabulary
- Listen for different purposes
- Develop auditory memory

Comprehension
- Recall details

Home–School Connection p.138
Spanish version available (see p. 2)

Circle Activity

Have students sit in a circle on the rug. Then connect the story to students' lives by asking:

> • *What are some fun things your family does together?*
> • *What is something new you would you like to do together?*

Introduce and model "Oh! Susanna." Have fun singing together, just as the family in the story does. After students know the words, have them clap along like the boy in the story.

> *I come from Alabama with my banjo on my knee;*
> *I'm going to Louisiana, my true love for to see.*
> *It rained all night the day I left, the weather it was dry;*
> *The sun so hot, I froze to death; Susanna, don't you cry.*
>
> *Oh, Susanna, Oh don't you cry for me.*
> *I come from Alabama with my banjo on my knee.*

Extend the Activity

Challenge students to listen carefully to the words in the song. They must "play a banjo" when they say the word **banjo** and then quickly slap their knees when they say the word **knee.**

Name _____

Family Night

Everyday Literacy: Listening and Speaking • EMC 2415 • © Evan-Moor Corp.

Name _____

Family Night

Did it happen in the story?

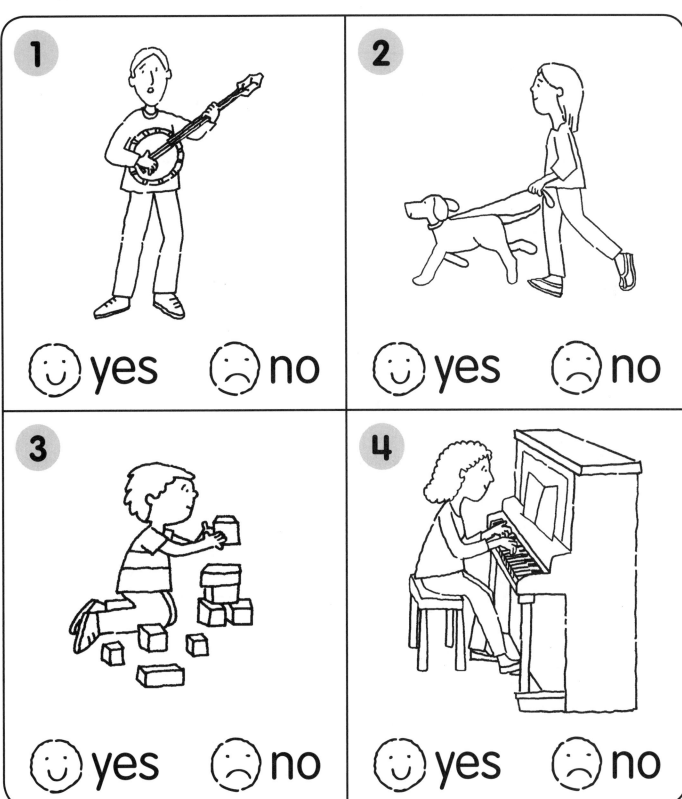

1. ☺ yes ☹ no
2. ☺ yes ☹ no
3. ☺ yes ☹ no
4. ☺ yes ☹ no

Name _____

Family Night

Let's clap rhythms together.

1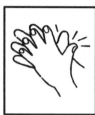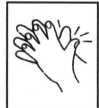

2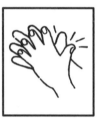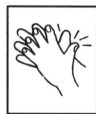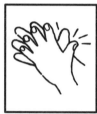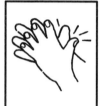

3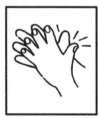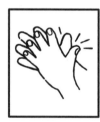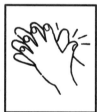

4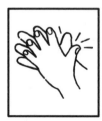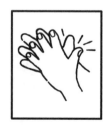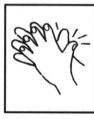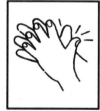

Everyday Literacy: Listening and Speaking • EMC 2415 • © Evan-Moor Corp.

Name _____

Family Night

What will happen next?

1

2
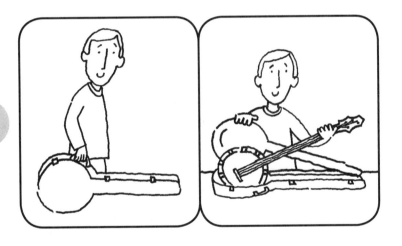

3

Name _____

What I Learned

To Parents

This week, your child listened to the story "Family Night." In the story, a family gets together every Tuesday night for family night. Often, they play music together. The mom, dad, sister, and brother all play instruments. The younger brother claps his hands and sings along. His favorite song is "Oh! Susanna."

What to Do

Have your child tell you what is happening in the picture. Ask questions such as: *Why is the family spending time together? What instruments are the family members playing? What song might the family be singing?* Encourage your child to use the vocabulary words in the box. Then have him or her color the picture.

Concept
Families have fun together.

Oral Vocabulary

banjo	play
clap	sing
family	song
music	

What to Do Next

Your child learned to sing "Oh! Susanna" this week. Sing it, or another favorite song, together.

Concept

Celebrate 100 days of school.

The 100th Day of School

Oral Vocabulary

Naming words: cereal, dots, necklace, sentence

Describing word: one hundred

Day 1

SKILLS:

Listening and Speaking
- Use new vocabulary
- Speak audibly
- Relate new vocabulary to prior knowledge
- Follow directions
- Take turns speaking in a group
- Respond appropriately to directions and questions
- Speak in complete sentences
- Interpret illustrations
- Identify a wide variety of objects

Comprehension
- Make inferences and draw conclusions
- Note details
- Recall details

Listening to the Story

Distribute the Day 1 picture to each student. Then read aloud the story below. Ask students to listen carefully as you read.

Today was the 100th day of Kindergarten. Our class celebrated by doing fun things. We made necklaces out of 100 cereal Os. We made pictures using 100 sticky dots. Then we went outside and everyone jumped 100 times and walked 100 steps. After we came inside, we were quiet for 100 seconds. My teacher helped me write my own sentence about the 100th day of Kindergarten. It said, "I wish I could eat 100 ice-cream cones today."

Making Inferences

Guide students in looking at the picture and discussing the story. Use the questions below to help students make connections and inferences.

- *What special day did the class celebrate?*
- *What did the students make?*
- *Do you think someone could really eat 100 ice-cream cones? Why or why not?*

Day 1 picture

Following Directions

Have students look at the picture. Then say:

Listen carefully and follow my directions.

- *How many days have the students been in Kindergarten?* (100) *What is the girl wearing around her neck?* (a necklace she made from 100 cereal Os) *What did you make on the 100th day of school?* (Answers vary.) *Make a brown dot on the girl's necklace. Make a blue dot on her shirt.*

- *What is the girl holding?* (a picture she made) *What did she use to make the picture?* (100 sticky dots) *What number is on the girl's headband?* (**100**) *Draw a green circle around the girl's picture. Use red to trace the number **100** on her headband.*

Have students color the picture.

SKILLS:

Listening and Speaking
- Speak in complete sentences
- Respond appropriately to directions and questions
- Interpret illustrations
- Describe people, places, things, locations, and actions
- Use new vocabulary
- Follow directions

Comprehension
- Recall details

Recalling the Story

Guide a discussion that helps students recall the Day 1 story. Reread the story if necessary. Say:

We listened to a story about the 100th day of school.

  • *What did the students do outside?*

Distribute the Day 2 activity. Then say:

Listen carefully and follow my directions.

  • *Look at box 1. What is the girl doing? (jumping) Did the students in the story jump? Color the happy face for **yes** or the sad face for **no**. (yes) How many times did the students jump? (100)*

  • *Look at box 2. What is the girl doing? (eating an ice-cream cone) Did the girl in the story want to eat an ice-cream cone? Color the happy face for **yes** or the sad face for **no**. (yes) How many ice-cream cones did she want to eat? (100)*

  • *Look at box 3. What is the girl doing? (making a necklace) Did the girl in the story use cereal to make a necklace? Color the happy face for **yes** or the sad face for **no**. (yes) How many cereal Os did she use to make her necklace? (100)*

  • *Look at box 4. What is the girl doing? (yelling) Did the students in the story yell? Color the happy face for **yes** or the sad face for **no**. (no) What did the students do after they came inside? (stayed quiet) For how many seconds were the students quiet? (100)*

Day 2 activity

SKILLS:

Listening and Speaking
- Listen for different purposes
- Identify a wide variety of objects
- Follow directions

Phonological Awareness
- Identify medial short vowel sounds in spoken words
- Perceive differences between similar-sounding spoken words

Listening for Short Vowel Sounds

Distribute the Day 3 activity. Then say:

Listen carefully and follow my directions. We're going to listen for the /ŏ/ sound.

  • *I will say a word. Listen for the middle sound: **hot**, /hŏt/. I hear the /ŏ/ sound in the middle of **hot**.*

  • *Name the pictures in box 1: **desk, dots**. Which word has the /ŏ/ sound? (**dots**) Draw a blue circle around the dots.*

  • *Name the pictures in box 2: **stop, stick**. Which word has the /ŏ/ sound? (**stop**) Draw a red circle around the stop sign.*

Day 3 activity

  • *Name the pictures in box 3: **clothes, clock**. Which word has the /ŏ/ sound? (**clock**) Draw a green circle around the clock.*

  • *Name the pictures in box 4: **mop, map**. Which word has the /ŏ/ sound? (**mop**) Draw a yellow circle around the mop.*

SKILLS:

Listening and Speaking
• Use new vocabulary
• Follow directions
• Speak in complete sentences
• Describe ideas, feelings, and experiences
• Take turns speaking in a group
• Speak audibly

Comprehension
• Recall details
• Respond to open-ended questions

Motor Skills
• Develop small muscle coordination

Finishing a Picture

Reread the Day 1 story if necessary. Say:

This week, our story was about what one class did on the 100th day of school.

  • *How did the students celebrate?*

  • *What did the girl's sentence say?*

Distribute the Day 4 activity. Then say:

Some things are missing on this page. Listen carefully and follow my directions.

  • *Find the face. Finish it to look like you. Draw eyes, a nose, a mouth, and hair.*

  • *If you could wish for 100 of something, what would you wish for?* (Answers vary.) *Draw a picture of what you would wish for in the big bubble.*

  • *The sentence below the picture says, "I wish I had 100…" Move your finger under the words and say them with me:* **I wish I had 100**… *Write the words that tell what you wished for.* (Assist students in completing the sentence.)

  • *Read your sentence to a partner.*

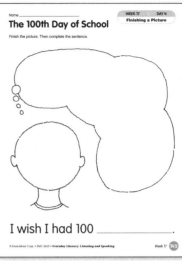

Day 4 activity

SKILLS:

Listening and Speaking
• Recite short poems, rhymes, and songs
• Take turns speaking in a group
• Respond appropriately to directions and questions
• Develop auditory memory

Comprehension
• Recall details

Circle Activity

Have students sit in a circle on the rug. Then review the concepts and vocabulary they practiced this week. Ask:

  • *What special day was it in the story?*

  • *What did the students make?*

  • *What did the class do outside?*

  • *What did the girl wish for?*

Teach students the song below, sung to the tune of "The Muffin Man." Model completing the sentence frames as you sing (e.g., balloons, diamonds, hamsters, pennies, elephants). Go around the room, with the class singing the song together, and each student taking a turn completing the sentence frames.

  Oh, I wish I had a hundred _____ (balloons),

  A hundred _____ (balloons), a hundred _____ (balloons).

  If I had a hundred _____ (balloons),

  I'd share them all with you.

Extend the Activity

Count to 100 with the students. You may also wish to create necklaces made of 100 cereal Os or pictures made with 100 stickers.

Home–School Connection p. 146
Spanish version available (see p. 2)

Name _____

The 100th Day of School

Name _____

The 100th Day of School

Did it happen in the story?

1 ☺ yes ☹ no

2 ☺ yes ☹ no

3 ☺ yes ☹ no

4 ☺ yes ☹ no

Name _____

The 100th Day of School

Listen for the /ŏ/ sound. Circle the picture.

Everyday Literacy: Listening and Speaking • EMC 2415 • © Evan-Moor Corp.

Name _____

The 100th Day of School

Finish the picture. Then complete the sentence.

I wish I had 100 _____.

Name ____________________

What I Learned

WEEK 17

Home–School Connection

Concept
Celebrate 100 days of school.

Oral Vocabulary

cereal
dots
necklace
one hundred
sentence

To Parents

This week, your child listened to the story "The 100th Day of School." In the story, a girl's Kindergarten class had fun making necklaces of 100 cereal Os and pictures from 100 sticky dots. Then the students went outside and jumped 100 times and walked 100 steps. After they went inside, the students were quiet for 100 seconds.

What to Do

Have your child tell you what is happening in the picture. Ask questions such as: ***What did the students in the story do on the 100th day of school? What do you wish you had 100 of? Can you count to 100?*** Encourage your child to use the vocabulary words in the box. Then have him or her color the picture.

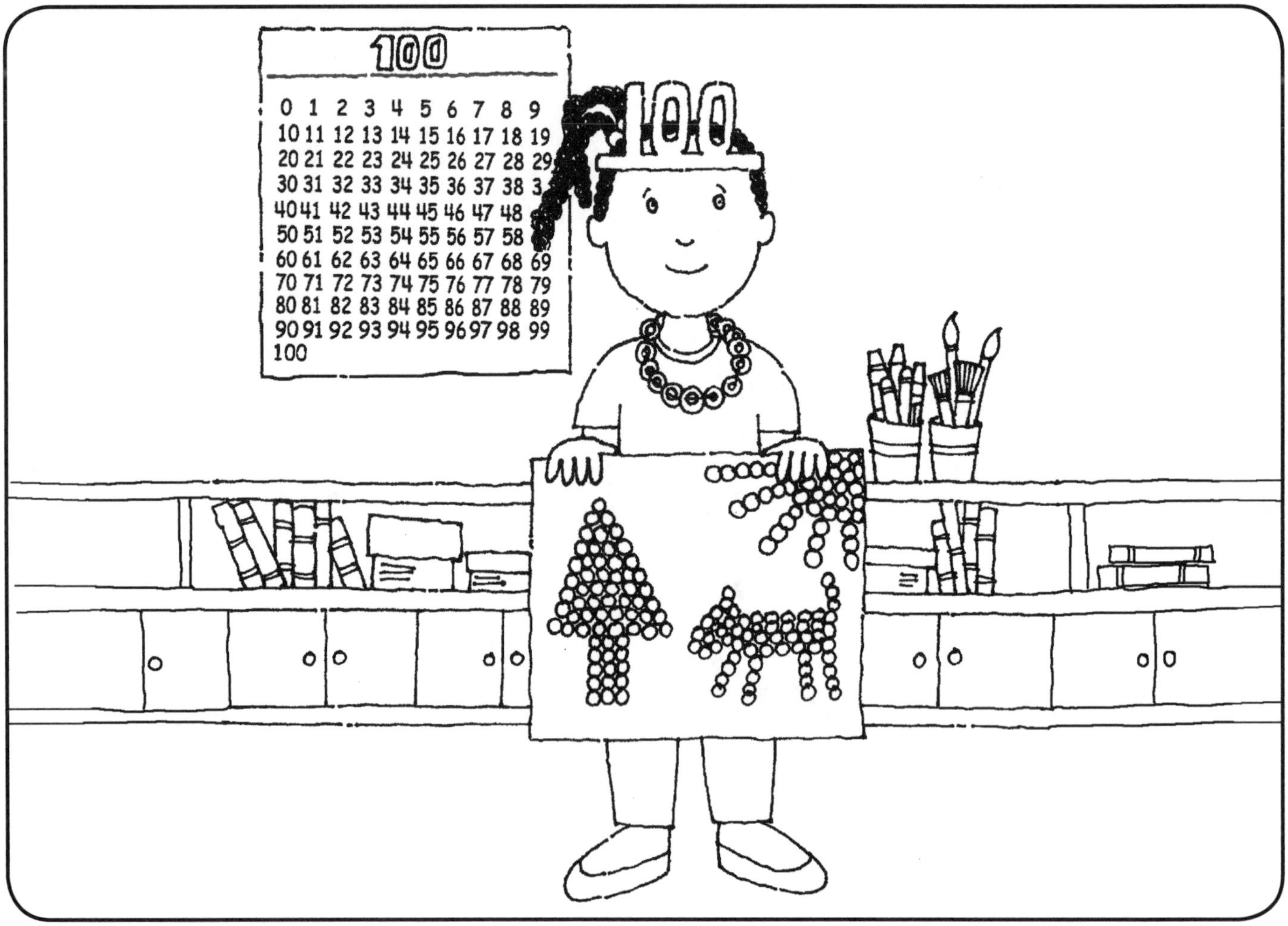

What to Do Next

Have your child count out 100 small items and place them in a sandwich bag (e.g., paper clips, cereal Os, pennies, pasta shells, toothpicks, etc.).

A tree has roots, a trunk, branches, and leaves.

Parts of a Tree

Oral Vocabulary

Naming words: branches, leaves, part, roots, tree, trunk

Day 1

SKILLS:

Listening and Speaking
- Speak in complete sentences
- Use new vocabulary
- Relate new vocabulary to prior knowledge
- Speak audibly
- Take turns speaking in a group
- Identify a wide variety of objects
- Follow directions
- Interpret illustrations
- Use language to show reasoning
- Respond appropriately to directions and questions

Comprehension
- Make inferences and draw conclusions
- Recall details

Listening to the Story

Distribute the Day 1 picture to each student. Then read aloud the story below. Ask students to listen carefully as you read.

We learned about the parts of a tree in school today. I made a picture that shows how all the parts work together to keep the tree alive. The roots of a tree keep the tree standing up by growing down into the soil. The roots also drink water from the soil. The water goes up the trunk and out to the leaves. The branches help by holding all the leaves. The leaves make food for the tree and send the food back down to the roots. A tree is an amazing living thing!

Making Inferences

Guide students in looking at the picture and discussing the story. Use the questions below to help students make connections and inferences.

- *Why is it important for the parts of a tree to work together?*
- *What do you think might happen if one tree part is not working?*

Following Directions

Have students look at the picture. Then say:
Listen carefully and follow my directions.

- *What do the roots of a tree do?* (keep tree standing up, drink water) *Draw a brown circle around the roots of the tree in the picture.*
- *What do the branches of a tree do?* (hold up the leaves) *Make a red dot on one of the branches on the tree.*
- *What do the leaves of a tree do?* (make food for the tree) *Make green dots on some leaves on the tree.*
- *Point to the trunk. The trunk connects the roots and leaves. Make a brown dot on the trunk.*

Have students color the picture according to the dots they made.

Day 1 picture

SKILLS:

Listening and Speaking
• Speak audibly
• Speak in complete sentences
• Respond appropriately to directions and questions
• Use language to show reasoning
• Use new vocabulary
• Interpret illustrations

Comprehension
• Make connections and draw inferences
• Recall details

Motor Skills
• Develop small muscle coordination

Labeling

Guide a discussion that helps students recall the Day 1 story. Reread the story if necessary. Say:

Our story was about a boy learning about trees.

  • *What four parts of a tree did the boy show in his picture?*

Distribute the Day 3 activity. Then say:

We're going to name the parts of a tree.

  • *Let's point to the same tree branch together. (Point to the branch that is labeled.) This is a tree branch. Now put your pencil on the word by the branch. This word says* **branch***. Trace the letters to write the word* **branch***.*

  • *Now let's point to the leaf that is labeled. Put your pencil on the word by the leaf. This word says* **leaf***. Trace the letters to write the word* **leaf***.*

  • *Now let's point to the trunk of the tree. Put your pencil on the word by the trunk. This word says* **trunk***. Trace the letters to write the word* **trunk***.*

  • *Now let's point to the root of the tree that is labeled. Put your pencil on the word by the root. This word says* **root***. Trace the letters to write the word* **root***.*

  • *Now point to each word and read it to a partner.*

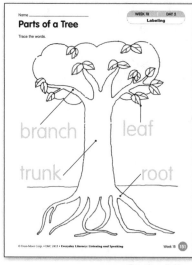

Day 2 activity

SKILLS:

Listening and Speaking
• Use new vocabulary
• Interpret illustrations
• Speak audibly
• Follow directions

Comprehension
• Recall details
• Make connections using illustrations and prior knowledge
• Respond to open-ended questions

Motor Skills
• Develop small muscle coordination

Drawing

Distribute the Day 3 activity. Then say:

The boy in the story thinks trees are amazing. Let's look at some things that trees do.

  • *Put your finger on the apple. Some trees grow food. Apple trees grow apples. Trees also grow fruits like oranges and lemons. This tree is an apple tree. Draw two apples on the tree.*

  • *Put your finger on the squirrel. Trees can be homes. Animals such as squirrels and birds live in trees. Draw a hole for the squirrel on the trunk of the tree. Draw a nest for the bird on the branches of the tree.*

  • *Can you name other things people and animals use trees for? (e.g., for shade, for wood to build things)*

Day 3 activity

SKILLS:

Listening and Speaking
• Use new vocabulary
• Identify a wide variety of objects
• Listen for different purposes

Comprehension
• Recall details

Phonological Awareness
• Blend the sounds of an onset/rime of a spoken word

Blending Onsets and Rimes

Reread the Day 1 story if necessary. Say:

Our story was about a boy who drew a tree.

• *What did he learn about trees?*

Distribute the Day 4 activity. Then say:

Listen carefully and follow my directions. I will say the beginning of a word and then the end of a word. Listen: b•oy. The word is **boy**.

• *Now it's your turn. Name the pictures in row 1. (* **boots**, **roof**, **roots***) Listen: r•oots. What is the word? (* **roots***) Circle the roots.*

• *Name the pictures in row 2. (* **food**, **foot**, **fish***) Listen: f•ood. What is the word? (* **food***) Circle the food.*

• *Name the pictures in row 3. (* **mop**, **dog**, **log***) Listen: l•og. What is the word? (* **log***) Circle the log.*

• *Name the pictures in row 4. (* **leaf**, **lamp**, **bee***) Listen: l•eaf. What is the word? (* **leaf***) Circle the leaf.*

Day 4 activity

SKILLS:

Listening and Speaking
• Speak in complete sentences
• Recite short poems, rhymes, and songs
• Use new vocabulary
• Follow directions
• Develop auditory memory

Comprehension
• Recall details

Motor Skills
• Develop large muscle coordination

Circle Activity

Have students sit in a circle on the rug. Then review the concepts and vocabulary they practiced this week. Ask:

• *What are the parts of a tree?*

• *What have you learned about trees? What do they do?*

Introduce and model the song below, sung to the tune of "The Farmer in the Dell." Have students stand in their circle. Lead them in doing the actions to demonstrate the parts of a tree.

(Spread fingers and touch the ground.)
My roots are underground, My roots are underground;
Hi-ho, the cherry-o, My roots are underground.

(Stand up straight and tall.)
My trunk stands straight and tall, My trunk stands straight and tall;
Hi-ho, the cherry-o, My trunk stands straight and tall.

(Lift arms high.)
My branches reach up high, My branches reach up high;
Hi-ho, the cherry-o, My branches reach up high.

(Lift arms, wiggle fingers.)
My leaves are growing there, My leaves are growing there;
Hi-ho, the cherry-o, My leaves are growing there.

Home–School Connection p. 154
Spanish version available (see p. 2)

Extend the Activity

Take students outside to look at different kinds of trees. See how many they can find. If possible, have students gather leaves to compare.

Name _____

Parts of a Tree

Everyday Literacy: Listening and Speaking • EMC 2415 • © Evan-Moor Corp.

Name _____

Parts of a Tree

Trace the words.

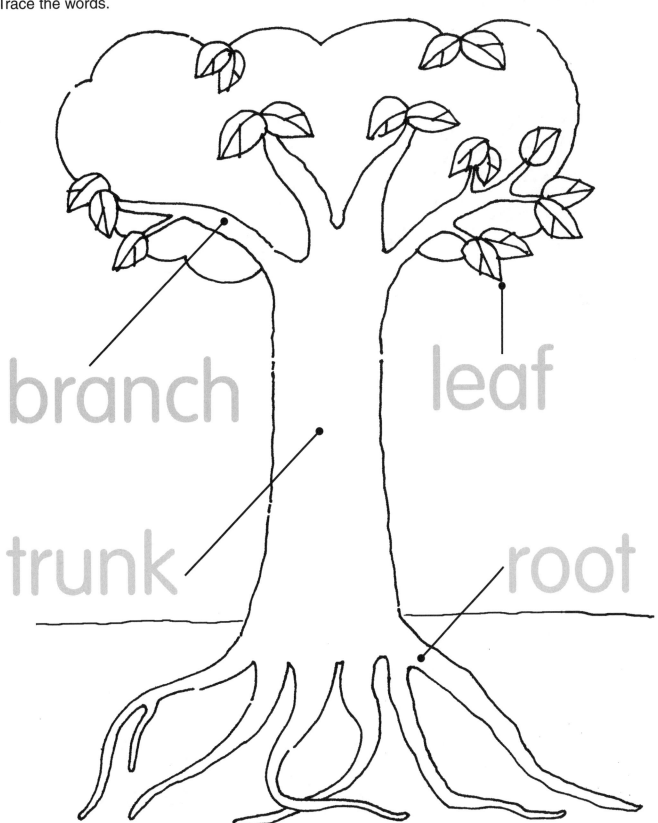

branch

leaf

trunk

root

Name _____

Parts of a Tree

Listen and follow the directions.

Everyday Literacy: Listening and Speaking • EMC 2415 • © Evan-Moor Corp.

Name _____

Parts of a Tree

Listen and circle the word you hear.

1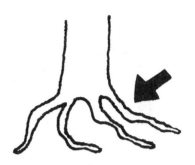

2

3

4

Name _____

What I Learned

To Parents

This week, your child listened to the story "Parts of a Tree." In the story, a boy learned about the parts of a tree. He made a picture to show how all the parts work together to keep the tree alive. The roots keep the tree standing up and drink water from the ground. The trunk sends the water to the leaves. The branches hold the leaves. The leaves make food for the tree. The boy thinks that trees are amazing living things!

Concept
A tree has roots, a trunk, branches, and leaves.

Oral Vocabulary
branches   roots
leaves   tree
part   trunk

What to Do

Have your child tell you about the picture. Ask questions such as:
What are the four parts of a tree? What do the roots do? The trunk? The branches? The leaves?
Encourage your child to use the vocabulary words in the box. Then have him or her color the picture.

What to Do Next

Have your child create a picture of a tree, using his or her choice of art materials. Then help your child label the four parts (roots, trunk, branches, leaves) by tracing letters you have written.

Classroom Zoo

Oral Vocabulary

Naming words: animals, lion, monkey, tiger, zoo

Day 1

SKILLS:

Listening and Speaking
- Speak in complete sentences
- Use new vocabulary
- Speak audibly
- Relate new vocabulary to prior knowledge
- Follow directions
- Listen for different purposes
- Interpret illustrations
- Respond appropriately to directions and questions
- Take turns speaking in a group

Comprehension
- Make inferences and draw conclusions
- Recall details
- Make connections using illustrations and prior knowledge

Listening to the Story

Distribute the Day 1 picture to each student. Then read aloud the story below. Ask students to listen carefully as you read.

Last week, we made a classroom zoo. First, we learned important information, or facts, about zoo animals. We looked in books and on the computer. Mrs. Diaz wrote the facts on a chart for us. Next, we made pictures of our zoo animals. I painted a lion. Emma drew a monkey. Ethan painted a tiger. On Friday, our families came to see our classroom zoo. We took turns showing our pictures and sharing facts about zoo animals.

Making Inferences

Guide students in looking at the picture and discussing the story. Use the questions below to help students make connections and inferences.

- *What is a zoo?*
- *What other animals live in zoos?*

Following Directions

Have students look at the picture. Then say:

Listen carefully and follow my directions.

Day 1 picture

- *Where was the students' zoo?* (in the classroom) *What did the students do first?* (learned facts about animals) *Where did they find the facts?* (from books and the computer) *Make a black dot on the computer. Make a red dot on the book about animals.*

- *What did the students do after Mrs. Diaz wrote down the facts?* (made pictures of their animals) *Make a yellow dot on the lion. Make a brown dot on the monkey. Make an orange dot on the tiger.*

- *What did the students do when their families came to the classroom zoo?* (showed their pictures and shared fatcs about their animals) *What animal did the girl who is standing learn about?* (lion) *Make a blue dot on the girl who is standing.*

Have students color the picture according to the dots they made.

SKILLS:

Listening and Speaking
- Speak audibly
- Respond appropriately to directions and questions
- Speak in complete sentences
- Use new vocabulary
- Follow directions
- Interpret illustrations

Comprehension
- Recall details

Recalling the Story

Guide a discussion that helps students recall the Day 1 story. Reread the story if necessary. Say:

We listened to a story about students who made a zoo in their classroom.

- *How did they make a classroom zoo?*

Distribute the Day 2 activity. Then say:

Listen carefully and follow my directions.

- *What do you see in box 1?* (children going to the zoo) *Did the students in the story go to the zoo? Color the happy face for* **yes** *or the sad face for* **no**. (no)

- *What do you see in box 2?* (a girl painting a picture of a lion) *Did one of the girls in the story paint a picture of a lion? Color the happy face for* **yes** *or the sad face for* **no**. (yes)

- *What do you see in box 3?* (a boy at a computer) *Did the students in the story use the computer to learn facts about zoo animals? Color the happy face for* **yes** *or the sad face for* **no**. (yes)

- *What do you see in box 4?* (a boy with a picture of a train) *Did the students in the story learn about a train? Color the happy face for* **yes** *or the sad face for* **no**. (no) *What did the children learn about?* (zoo animals)

Day 2 activity

SKILLS:

Listening and Speaking
- Follow directions
- Listen for different purposes
- Speak audibly

Phonological Awareness
- Break a spoken word into separate phonemes
- Identify and count phonemes

Comprehension
- Recall details

Listening for Phonemes

Reread the Day 1 story if necessary. Say:

Our story was about a classroom zoo.

- *What animals did the students learn about?*

Distribute the Day 3 activity. Then say:

Let's count how many sounds we hear in words.

- *Listen:* **paint**, /p-ā-n-t/. *I hear four sounds in the word* **paint**. *Now it's your turn.*

- *Look at box 1. This picture shows a zoo. Stretch the word* **zoo**, *sound by sound:* /z-oo/. *How many sounds do you hear?* (two) *Circle the number* **2** *under the zoo.*

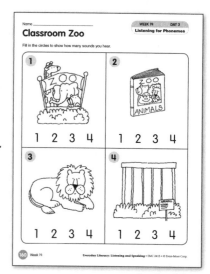

- *The picture in box 2 shows a book. Stretch the word* **book**, *sound by sound:* /b-oo-k/. *How many sounds do you hear?* (three) *Circle the number* **3** *under the book.*

- *Name the picture in box 3.* (lion) *Stretch the word* **lion**, *sound by sound:* /l-ī-ŏ-n/. *How many sounds do you hear?* (four) *Circle the number* **4** *under the lion.*

- *The picture in box 4 shows a cage. Stretch the word* **cage**, *sound by sound:* /k-ā-j/. *How many sounds do you hear?* (three) *Circle the number* **3** *under the cage.*

Day 3 activity

SKILLS:

Listening and Speaking
- Speak in complete sentences
- Use new vocabulary
- Relate new vocabulary to prior knowledge
- Follow directions
- Respond appropriately to directions and questions
- Listen critically to interpret and evaluate
- Identify a wide variety of objects
- Use language to show reasoning

Comprehension
- Categorize and classify
- Recall details
- Respond to open-ended questions

Motor Skills
- Develop small muscle coordination

Categorizing

Reread the Day 1 story if necessary. Say:

This week, our story was about students who made a zoo in their classroom.

- *Have you ever been to a zoo? What animals did you see?*

Distribute the Day 4 activity. Then say:

Listen carefully and follow my directions.

Day 4 activity

- *Let's draw a path through the zoo. Put your crayon on the zoo sign. Draw a line along the path to the tiger. Do some tigers live in zoos?* (yes) *Draw a circle around the tiger.*

- *Put your crayon back on the path where you stopped. Draw a line along the path again. What animal do you come to next?* (a dog) *Would a dog live in a zoo?* (no) *Where would a dog live?* (at a house)

- *Draw a line along the path again. What animal do you come to next?* (a lion) *Do some lions live in zoos?* (yes) *Draw a circle around the lion.*

- *Draw a line along the path again. What do you come to next?* (a snowman) *Would you see a snowman in a zoo?* (no) *Where might you see a snowman?* (in a yard; in the snow)

- *Draw a line along the path again. What animal do you come to next?* (a monkey) *Do some monkeys live in zoos?* (yes) *Draw a circle around the monkey.*

- *Draw a line along the path again. What do you come to last?* (children) *Would you see children in a zoo? Why?* (Yes. They visit the animals.) *Draw a circle around the children.*

Day 5

SKILLS:

Listening and Speaking
- Develop auditory memory
- Use new vocabulary
- Recite short poems, rhymes, and songs

Comprehension
- Recall details

Home–School Connection p. 162
Spanish version available (see p. 2)

Circle Activity

Have students sit in a circle on the rug. Then connect the story to students' lives by saying:

- *Pretend we are making a classroom zoo. What animals would be in our zoo? What facts do we know about those animals?*

Introduce the chant below by reading the first line and having the class echo you. Then model completing the sentence frame using the name of a zoo animal. Go around the circle, with the class chanting the first line together and having each student take a turn completing the sentence frame.

Chant together: *What did you see at the zoo, at the zoo?*

Student: *I saw a _____, how about you?*

Extend the Activity

Have students pat their knees and clap their hands to the rhythm of the words.

Name _____

Classroom Zoo

Everyday Literacy: Listening and Speaking • EMC 2415 • © Evan-Moor Corp.

Name _____

Classroom Zoo

Did it happen in the story?

1   😊 yes   ☹ no

2   😊 yes   ☹ no

3   😊 yes   ☹ no

4   😊 yes   ☹ no

Name _____

Classroom Zoo

Circle to show how many sounds you hear.

1

1   2   3   4

2

1   2   3   4

3

1   2   3   4

4

1   2   3   4

Name _____

Classroom Zoo

Circle the things that you would see at a zoo.

Name _____

What I Learned

To Parents

This week, your child listened to the story "Classroom Zoo." In the story, students made a classroom zoo. They researched animal facts in books and on the computer. The teacher wrote the facts on a chart. Then the students painted and drew pictures of animals for the classroom zoo. The students' families came to see the classroom zoo and listen to the students share facts about zoo animals.

Concept
Books and computers help us learn.

Oral Vocabulary

animals	tiger
lion	zoo
monkey	

What to Do

Have your child tell you what is happening in the picture. Ask questions such as: *What did the students make? How did the students learn about the animals? What animals do you see in the picture?* Encourage your child to use the vocabulary words in the box. Then have him or her color the picture.

What to Do Next

Help your child find pictures of animals in books, magazines, or on the computer. Have your child compare the animals. Ask questions such as: *Which animals have fur? Which animals have feathers? Which ones are fierce? Which ones are friendly? Which ones can be found at a zoo?*

WEEK 20

A New Friend

Oral Vocabulary

Naming words: friend, lizard, swing, tail
Action words: scurry, sneeze, watch
Describing words: green, tiny

Concept
Watch living things to learn about them.

Day 1

SKILLS:

Listening and Speaking
• Speak audibly
• Speak in complete sentences
• Use new vocabulary
• Relate new vocabulary to prior knowledge
• Take turns speaking in a group
• Follow directions
• Describe people, places, things, locations, and actions
• Use language to show reasoning
• Describe ideas, feelings, and experiences

Comprehension
• Make inferences and draw conclusions
• Make predictions
• Determine cause and effect
• Respond to open-ended questions
• Recall details
• Make connections using illustrations and real-life experiences

Listening to the Story

Distribute the Day 1 picture to each student. Then read aloud the story below. Ask students to listen carefully as you read.

I found a new friend on the playground today. He was sitting on a swing. He was tiny and green, with brown stripes and a long tail. His head looked like an alligator's head. I watched him very quietly. But when I sneezed, he scurried away and disappeared under the fence. My new friend is shy, but I'm hoping he'll come back tomorrow. I'll be watching for him.

Making Inferences

Guide students in looking at the picture and discussing the story. Use the questions below to help students make connections and inferences.

- *Who was the new friend on the playground?*
- *What happened to make the lizard disappear under the fence?*
- *Do you think the lizard will be back? Why or why not?*

Day 1 picture

Following Directions

Have students look at the picture. Then say:

Listen carefully and follow my directions.

- *What did the boy find on the playground?* (a new friend, a tiny lizard) *Where was the lizard?* (sitting on a swing) *What did it look like?* (tiny, green, stripes, long tail, alligator head) *Make an orange dot on the swing. Make a green dot on the lizard.*

- *What did the lizard do when the boy sneezed?* (It scurried away and disappeared under the fence.) *What will the boy do tomorrow?* (look for the lizard on the playground) *Make a brown dot on the boy. Make a blue dot on the fence.*

- *Have you ever seen a lizard? What did it look like?* (Answers vary.)

Have students color the picture according to the dots they made.

Day 2

SKILLS:

Listening and Speaking
- Speak in complete sentences
- Use new vocabulary
- Interpret illustrations
- Follow directions
- Respond appropriately to directions and questions

Comprehension
- Recall details
- Identify a sequence of events
- Retell a story

Sequencing

Guide a discussion that helps students recall the Day 1 story. Reread the story if necessary. Say:

In our story, a boy found a new friend.

- *Where was the lizard?*
- *What other animal did the lizard look like?*

Distribute the Day 2 activity. Then say:

These pictures show what happened in our story. Let's put them in the order they happened.

- *Which picture shows what happened first? (a boy watching a lizard) Draw a line from the picture to the number 1.*
- *Which picture shows what happened next? (a boy sneezing) Draw a line from that picture to the number 2.*
- *Which picture shows what happened last? (the lizard running under the fence) Draw a line from that picture to the number 3.*
- *Think about what a lizard looks like. Draw a lizard in the box.*

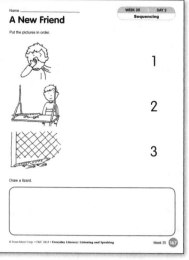

Day 2 activity

Day 3

SKILLS:

Listening and Speaking
- Use new vocabulary
- Follow directions
- Listen for different purposes
- Identify a wide variety of objects

Comprehension
- Recall details

Phonological Awareness
- Recognize words that rhyme
- Perceive differences between similar-sounding spoken words

Listening for Rhyme

Reread the Day 1 story if necessary. Say:

Our story was about a lizard on the playground.

- *Why was the boy quiet while he watched the lizard?*

Distribute the Day 3 activity. Then say:

Listen carefully and follow my directions.

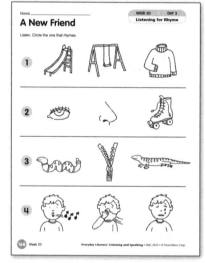

Day 3 activity

- *Look at the pictures in row 1. Listen for words that rhyme with **sing**. **Sing**, **slide**; do these words rhyme? (no) **Sing**, **swing**; do these words rhyme? (yes) Circle the swing. **Sing**, **sweater**; do these words rhyme? (no).*
- *Look at the pictures in row 2. Listen for words that rhyme with **sky**. **Sky**, **eye**; do these words rhyme? (yes) Circle the eye. **Sky**, **nose**; do these words rhyme? (no) **Sky**, **skate**; do these words rhyme? (no)*
- *Look at the pictures in row 3. Listen for words that rhyme with **blizzard**. **Blizzard**, **snake**; do these words rhyme? (no) **Blizzard**, **zipper**; do these words rhyme? (no) **Blizzard**, **lizard**; do these words rhyme? (yes) Circle the lizard.*
- *Look at the pictures in row 4. Listen for words that rhyme with **keys**. **Keys**, **sing**; do these words rhyme? (no) **Keys**, **sneeze**; do these words rhyme? (yes) Circle the boy sneezing. **Sneeze**, **cry**; do these words rhyme? (no)*

Everyday Literacy: Listening and Speaking • EMC 2415 • © Evan-Moor Corp.

Finishing a Picture

Reread the Day 1 story if necessary. Say:

This week, our story was about a boy who saw a lizard on the playground.

- *Why did the lizard scurry under the fence?*
- *What would you do if you saw a lizard on the playground?*

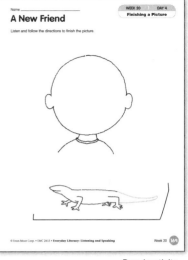

Day 4 activity

Distribute the Day 4 activity. Then say:

Some things are missing from the picture on this page. Listen carefully and follow my directions.

- *Point to the lizard. The lizard needs a tail. What kind of tail did the lizard in our story have?* (long) *Use green to trace the lizard's long tail. Then make a black dot for the lizard's eye.*
- *What color was the lizard in our story?* (green) *Color the lizard green. Then draw three brown stripes on its back.*
- *Where was the lizard sitting in our story?* (on a swing) *Draw the swing under the lizard.*
- *Finish drawing the face to look like you. Draw eyes, a nose, a mouth, and hair.*

Circle Activity

Have students sit in a circle on the rug. Then connect the story to students' lives by asking:

- *Where have you seen a lizard?*
- *Have you ever touched a lizard? How did it feel?*

Introduce the chant below by reading the first two lines and having the class echo you. Then model how to complete the sentence frame, using an animal name. As the class recites the chant, allow each student to complete the sentence frame.

Chant together: *Who did you meet on the playground today?*
Who did you greet when you went out to play?

Student: *I met a _____ on the playground today.*
(lizard, alligator, bear, etc.)

Extend the Activity

Have students say the name of a classmate as you chant around the circle (e.g., "I met Emily on the playground today."). Make it a rule that once a name is called, it cannot be called again.

Name _____

A New Friend

Name _____

A New Friend

Put the pictures in order.

 3

Draw a lizard.

Name _____

A New Friend

Listen. Circle the one that rhymes.

1

2

3

4

Name _____

A New Friend

Listen and follow the directions to finish the picture.

Name _____

What I Learned

To Parents

This week, your child listened to the story "A New Friend." In the story, a boy met a new friend on the playground—a lizard. The boy watched the lizard quietly, but when he sneezed, the lizard scurried away and disappeared under the fence. The boy hopes the lizard will be back another day.

What to Do

Have your child tell you about the story below. Point to one picture at a time and have him or her explain what is happening. Encourage your child to use vocabulary words in the box. Then have him or her color the pictures.

Concept
Watch living things to learn about them.

Oral Vocabulary

friend	sneeze
green	swing
lizard	tail
scurry	tiny

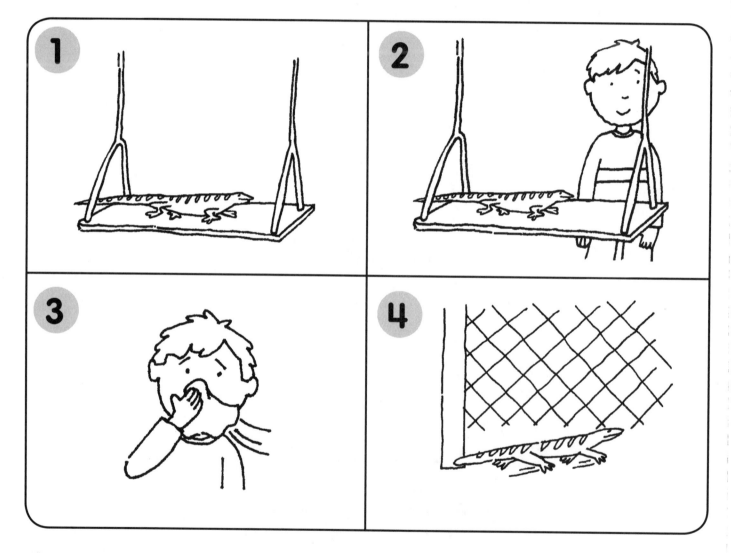

What to Do Next

Help your child cut apart the four pictures on this page. Play a game by mixing up the pieces and having him or her put them back into the correct story order. Have your child tell the story to other family members.

Everyday Literacy: Listening and Speaking • EMC 2415 • © Evan-Moor Corp.

Answer Key

Week 1

Day 2
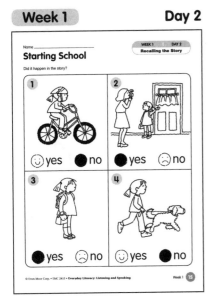

Day 3

Day 4
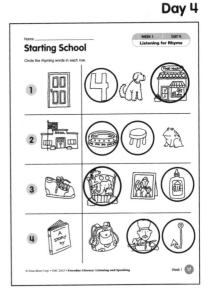

Week 2

Day 2
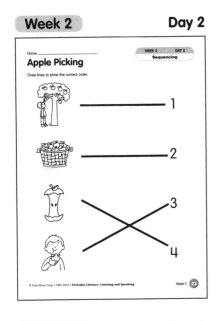

Day 3

Day 4

Week 3

Day 2

Day 3

Day 4

Week 4

Day 2

Name _____
Fall Fun

WEEK 4   DAY 2
Identifying Pictures

Listen and follow the directions.

1. ● yes ☹ no
2. ● yes ☹ no
3. ☺ yes ● no
4. ● yes ☹ no

© Evan-Moor Corp. • EMC 2415 • **Everyday Literacy: Listening and Speaking** Week 4 39

Day 3

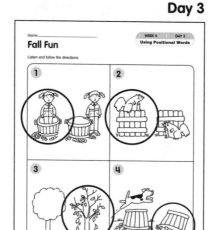

Name _____
Fall Fun

WEEK 4   DAY 3
Using Positional Words

Listen and follow the directions.

40 Week 4 **Everyday Literacy: Listening and Speaking** • EMC 2415 • © Evan-Moor Corp.

Day 4

Name _____
Fall Fun

WEEK 4   DAY 4
Listening for Ending Sounds

Circle the picture that has the same ending sound.

© Evan-Moor Corp. • EMC 2415 • **Everyday Literacy: Listening and Speaking** Week 4 41

Week 5

Day 2

Name _____
Winter Weather

WEEK 5   DAY 2
Recalling the Story

Did it happen in the story?

1. ● yes ☹ no
2. ☺ yes ● no
3. ● yes ☹ no
4. ☺ yes ● no

© Evan-Moor Corp. • EMC 2415 • **Everyday Literacy: Listening and Speaking** Week 5 47

Day 3

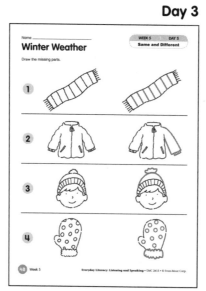

Name _____
Winter Weather

WEEK 5   DAY 3
Same and Different

Draw the missing parts.

48 Week 5 **Everyday Literacy: Listening and Speaking** • EMC 2415 • © Evan-Moor Corp.

Day 4

Name _____
Winter Weather

WEEK 5   DAY 4
Identifying Seasons

Listen and follow the directions.

© Evan-Moor Corp. • EMC 2415 • **Everyday Literacy: Listening and Speaking** Week 5 49

Week 6

Day 2

Name _____
Spring Is Here

WEEK 6   DAY 2
Categorizing

Listen and follow the directions.

1. green   green
2. yellow
3. blue
4. purple

© Evan-Moor Corp. • EMC 2415 • **Everyday Literacy: Listening and Speaking** Week 6 55

Day 3

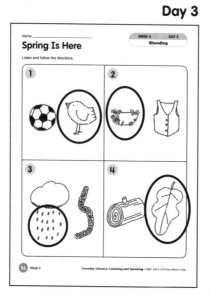

Name _____
Spring Is Here

WEEK 6   DAY 3
Blending

Listen and follow the directions.

56 Week 6 **Everyday Literacy: Listening and Speaking** • EMC 2415 • © Evan-Moor Corp.

Day 4

Name _____
Spring Is Here

WEEK 6   DAY 4
Finishing a Picture

Listen and draw.

purple

spring

© Evan-Moor Corp. • EMC 2415 • **Everyday Literacy: Listening and Speaking** Week 6 57

Drawings vary.

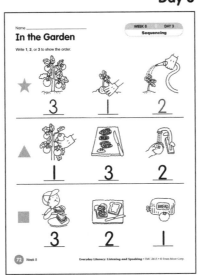

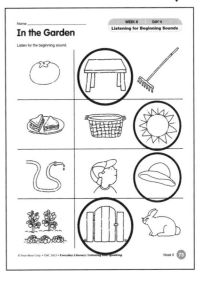

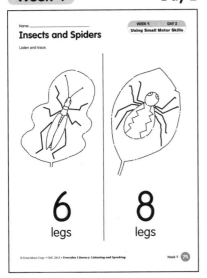

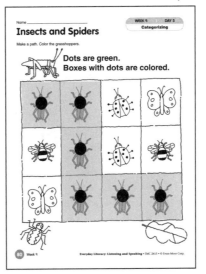

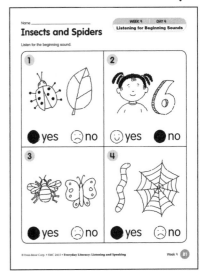

Week 10

Day 2

Fire Safety

WEEK 10   DAY 2
Recalling the Story

Listen and follow the directions.

1. red
2. blue
3. black
4. green

© Evan-Moor Corp. • EMC 2415 • Everyday Literacy: Listening and Speaking   Week 10   87

Day 3

Fire Safety

WEEK 10   DAY 3
Using Small Motor Skills

Listen and trace.

stop

drop

roll

88   Week 10   Everyday Literacy: Listening and Speaking • EMC 2415 • © Evan-Moor Corp.

Day 4

Fire Safety

WEEK 10   DAY 4
Listening for Consonant Sounds

Listen and follow the directions.

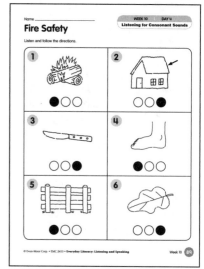

© Evan-Moor Corp. • EMC 2415 • Everyday Literacy: Listening and Speaking   Week 10   89

Week 11

Day 2

The Lion and the Mouse

WEEK 11   DAY 2
Retelling a Story

Finish the pictures. Tell the story.

1
2
3
4. end

© Evan-Moor Corp. • EMC 2415 • Everyday Literacy: Listening and Speaking   Week 11   95

Day 3

The Lion and the Mouse

WEEK 11   DAY 3
Blending Syllables

Listen to the word parts. Circle the answer.

96   Week 11   Everyday Literacy: Listening and Speaking • EMC 2415 • © Evan-Moor Corp.

Day 4

The Lion and the Mouse

WEEK 11   DAY 4
Using Word Opposites

Listen and follow the directions.

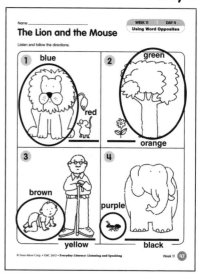

1. blue / red
2. green / orange
3. brown / yellow
4. purple / black

© Evan-Moor Corp. • EMC 2415 • Everyday Literacy: Listening and Speaking   Week 11   97

Week 12

Day 2

Family Picnic

WEEK 12   DAY 2
Recalling the Story

Did it happen in the story?

1. yes / no
2. yes / no
3. yes / no
4. yes / no

© Evan-Moor Corp. • EMC 2415 • Everyday Literacy: Listening and Speaking   Week 12   103

Day 3

Family Picnic

WEEK 12   DAY 3
Listening for Phonemes

Listen and follow the directions.

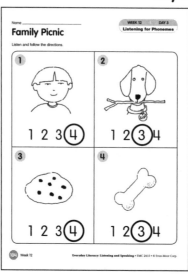

1. 1 2 3 (4)
2. 1 2 (3) 4
3. 1 2 3 (4)
4. 1 2 (3) 4

104   Week 12   Everyday Literacy: Listening and Speaking • EMC 2415 • © Evan-Moor Corp.

Day 4

Family Picnic

WEEK 12   DAY 4
Using Auditory Memory

Listen and follow the directions.

1
2
3
4

© Evan-Moor Corp. • EMC 2415 • Everyday Literacy: Listening and Speaking   Week 12   105

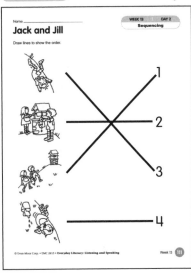

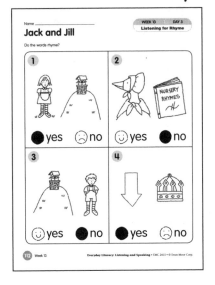

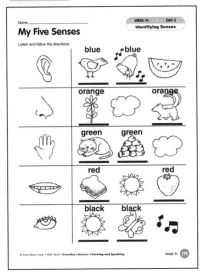

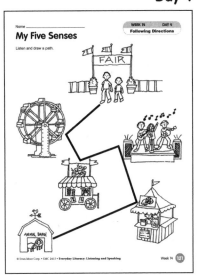

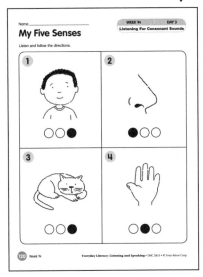

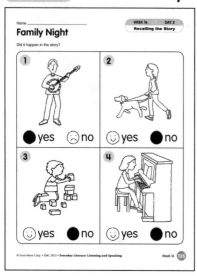

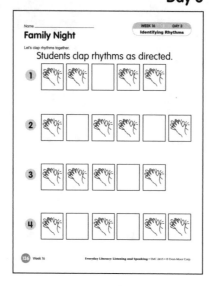

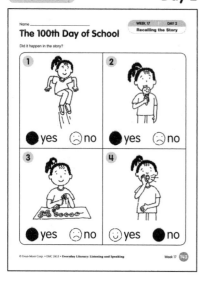

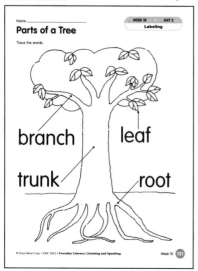